My friend Paul Powers [was one]
of the most pathetic victi[ms of]
child abuse I've ever known. . . .
Paul's story touched me deeply
and will, I know, be inspirational
to others.

Dr. James Dobson
Love Must Be Tough

Distributed By:
Morning Rose Publishers
P.O. Box 64003, RPO Clarke Road
Coquitlam, B.C. V3J 7V6 CANADA

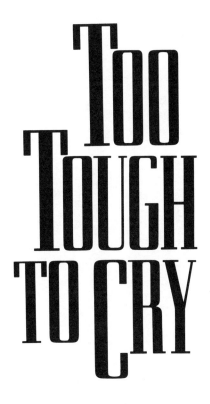

TOO TOUGH TO CRY

PAUL POWERS
with Fritz Ridenour

To Christ love

Paul Powers

Rom 10:20

ACKNOWLEDGMENTS

I would like to make special note
of the following people for their
unique role in my life:

Geoff and Beverly Still
who for many, many years
listened to, guided, supported,
and loved our family

Dr. James Dobson
who encouraged me to make full use
of the potential God has given

Fritz Ridenour
who has looked inside of me
as no other has ever done

Front cover photo by Robert Phillips

This biography contains many actual names and
places, but some names have been changed to
protect privacy.

Unless otherwise noted, all Scripture quotations
are from the *Holy Bible,* King James Version.
Scripture quotations marked NIV are from the *Holy
Bible,* New International Version, copyright © 1973,
1978, 1984 International Bible Society. Used by
permission of Zondervan Bible Publishers.

Library of Congress Catalog Card Number 90-70194
ISBN 0-8423-7286-5
Copyright © 1990 by Paul Powers and Fritz Ridenour
All rights reserved
Printed in Canada

96 95 94
9   8   7   6   5   4   3   2

To Clarence and Clara Adams
whose memory will always remind me
of family, forgiveness, and love

CONTENTS

1

ONE
THE GOLDEN BOX

Shivering in the December cold but burning with anger inside, I wearily trudged up the walk of my home in a Toronto suburb. I had spent the most humiliating day of my life—begging churches for money they owed me!

Finances were tight that holiday season of 1972. My wife, Margie, and two daughters, Christina, four, and Paula, not quite two, faced a bleak Christmas. Throughout the fall I had done children's crusades in at least eight churches in the Toronto area, but none had paid me at the time I spoke.

"We'll send you the offering in the mail," was the usual excuse. "We have to put it through our books first."

We had waited and waited, but no checks had come. Margie was pushing me for more money so she could get some of the household bills off of her mind. We had business creditors who needed to be paid, and we also owed Margie's parents a sizeable amount of money they had loaned us earlier that year.

As Christmas approached I got more and more frustrated and angry. I was sitting there one day, muttering about Christians who didn't pay their bills, when Margie said, "Well, stop complaining. Why don't you just go to the churches and tell them the truth? We need the money!"

It was December 23, and after breakfast I had driven to the churches that were closest to our home, talking to pastors and church secretaries, but always the answer was the same: "The check should be in the mail. Perhaps the mail strike held it up."

Or, "I'm not sure about your check—I think it's waiting to be approved by the church treasurer."

"Look," I told the secretary at one church, "I'm practically broke. All I'm asking for is what the church owes me so my wife and two little girls can have a decent Christmas."

She opened the cash box in her desk drawer and took out a few dollars, saying, "I'm sorry, Mr. Powers, it's all I can give you without authorization from the pastor, but he won't be back until tomorrow night."

I had replayed this same humiliating scenario all day long, getting a few dollars here and there, but no full payment from anyone. Instead, I often got looks that seemed to say, *You're in God's business—don't you trust God to provide?*

As I drove home I thought, *Yes, God does provide—he provides through his people, but if his people don't pay their debts, what then?* Along with the humiliation and anger, I felt spiritually dry and brittle. At Margie's insistence, I had been doing more speaking in churches instead of the magic acts in secular settings that always paid well. And now what did I have to show for it? We had very little food in the house—in fact, lately Margie and I had been joining the girls in eating pabulum because it was all we could afford.

At least tonight we'll have a decent meal, I told myself. *And when we get to the folks' farm on Christmas Eve, we'll eat like kings.*

Margie heard me come in and asked eagerly, "How did you do?"

"Not very well. I went to eight different churches and collected less than forty dollars. I got gas for the trip to the farm. Here's some money for groceries and whatever else you need to pick up. Spend it carefully, Margie; it's all we've got."

Margie hid her disappointment and tried to maintain her usual cheery attitude as she bundled up the girls and they left to go shopping. She was glad to get out of there. I had been gone far longer than she had planned, and now I had come home frustrated and fuming—ready to blow up. As she left, I was literally looking around the living room to see what we might take to the pawnshop.

About two hours later, Margie and the kids returned, chattering excitedly about what they had bought. Margie was feeling good about some bargains she'd found at Christmas sales, but all I said was, "You're kidding! We can't afford to buy much more than a few groceries."

Margie stiffened and said coolly, "I spent the money on what I thought we needed."

I continued grumbling as we put things away, and then Tina showed me a roll of gold wrapping paper. "Look what Mommy got, Daddy."

I took the roll of paper, looked at it, and said, "What kind of special bargain is this?"

"Mommy got it for a dollar," said Tina proudly.

"A dollar! Well, I hope it's enough paper to wrap all the presents," was all I could think of. It turned out to be far less than that—just one sheet on a cardboard roll. And it had cost one entire dollar!

All the anger and frustration of the day boiled up in me and spilled out all over everyone.

"How could you be so wasteful?" I screamed at Margie. "You've simply thrown away a whole dollar on nothing—nothing but stupid wrapping paper! How could you do such a thing, Margie? I've been rationing dimes and nickels for weeks, just to have some money for gas to drive to the farm for Christmas."

Margie didn't say anything. She just looked crushed. Tina tried to look away and act as if nothing had happened.

A cold, depressing cloud hung over the dinner table that evening. With the groceries she had purchased, Margie was able to fix a fine meal, but everyone sat in stoic silence, barely picking at the food. Heads and shoulders sagged under the weight of my frustration and angry words. At one point Tina lifted her tearful blue eyes, surveyed my face, and then looked down at her plate again.

After dinner we went downstairs to the bottom floor of our duplex where I had my office. We had to finish some last-minute gift wrapping and other final preparations before leaving the next day to spend Christmas with Margie's family. Tina was there with us, but because I didn't want her to see us wrapping the dolls we had gotten at a bargain sale earlier in the year, I sent her out saying, "Tina, would you go upstairs and get that gold paper your mother wasted the money on?"

I'm sure Tina didn't catch the full meaning of what I said, but Margie did. Margie knew I was trying to cut her down to size for being so "wasteful." Tina dutifully scampered off to find the paper while Margie and I continued wrapping presents, all the while bickering and picking at each other. I hadn't cut her down to size at all; I'd only undermined my own credibility as a husband and father. She defended her womanliness and right to buy what she felt was needed, and, of course, I defended my manliness by letting her know she was a bad manager.

"Oh yes, Paul," she snapped back. "You've got all the answers, don't you? You know everything."

Because Tina hadn't come back, I called upstairs but heard no answer.

"What's taking that kid so long?" I muttered as I stormed up the stairs with Margie right behind me. We came upon Tina in an alcove just off the living room, sitting in the middle of the floor, surrounded by wads of gold paper and three pairs of scissors. Gobs of sticky clear plastic tape were all over her as well as the rug. She had used up the entire single sheet of gold paper trying to wrap something that looked like a shoe box.

Tina smiled cheerfully as she saw us enter the room, but her smile turned to a look of terror as she saw the anger flooding my face. She sat wide-eyed and gave a pathetic little screech as I raced across the room, grabbed her by one arm, and jerked her right up into the air, slapping her hard several times.

Tina screamed in pain and terror as Margie stood there, horrified shock on her face. My head was spinning and I was practically incoherent, but Tina's screams and sobs made me realize what I was doing, and I stopped slapping her. My entire body began to shake, and suddenly other sounds flooded my mind—shouts of rage, anger, and pain that were locked in my memories of childhood. My thoughts flashed back to the innumerable times *I* had been the terrified child in the hands of a raging, drunken father.

I let go of Tina and she fell to the floor in a heap, still crying and really hurt by the jerking and slapping I had given her. Then I turned to Margie and tried to put the blame on her.

"Well, she deserved to be punished," I snapped. "And you know you shouldn't have wasted money on that wrapping paper." I sent Tina to her room as Margie stood there, still in shock. She couldn't believe this was happening. Here was the man she had married, the man who had said he loved Christ and children. The man who had thanked God for being given a children's ministry. Now he was acting like someone possessed by a demon, terrorizing his own child and leaving her with bruises and handprints on her cheek where he had struck her.

Guilt flooded in and seemed to drown me in waves of remorse. *See,* the old memories whispered. *You're just like your old man . . . just like your no-good, drunken father who beat you and your brothers and sisters. You're a failure. You've failed in everything you've tried, and now you're going to fail just like your dad did when your mom died. Now you're beating your child, smashing her, throwing her around, and shouting, just the way he used to do with you.*

Despite the guilt, I didn't apologize to anyone. Tina had been wrong; she had to learn. And Margie had to know I was head of the house. She had to learn her place and that I had the right to discipline the children. But even as I justified my position to Margie my mind kept telling me, *You liar, you hypocrite . . . haven't been set free from anything. You're living a fool's lie. You're just as bad as your father was, and you've been trying to fool everybody. The real Paul Powers is a guy who beats children just as his father did.*

For the rest of the evening, our home was colder than the brisk December night outside. Tina stayed in her room, and Margie wouldn't even talk to me. Later I went in to talk to Tina, who was still wide awake and looking frightened and sad at the same time. What I said didn't comfort her: "How could you do such a stupid thing? Don't you know how hard I worked for this money? You know I was gone almost all day, just for a few crummy bucks! How dare you! Aren't you sorry for what you did with the wrapping paper?"

Tina looked up at me and said in a tiny, trembling voice, "Yes, Daddy, I'm s-s-sorry."

I didn't even kiss her good night. My arrogant pride just wouldn't let me. I spent the night on the couch down in my office. Margie had stood at the door to Tina's room and heard my "good night" tirade. She didn't want anything to do with me—and I didn't blame her. I tossed and turned all night long, never really falling asleep, only hearing the voices saying, *You're just like your father . . . you're a coward who beats little children . . . just like your father . . . you're no good, no good, no good . . .*

The next morning was the twenty-fourth, and we tried to begin the day as we always do—by having devotions and thanking the Lord. But the words stuck in my mouth, and my hurried prayer definitely bounced off the ceiling. Margie was barely talking to me, but I still wasn't ready to apologize. I loved Margie, but my pride stood between us.

We were due to leave around ten, and we decided to go ahead and give the girls their dolls, which we had wrapped the night before. That way they would have something to play with on the hundred-mile drive to the farm. The girls opened their gifts at the breakfast table with squeals of delight. They seemed to have forgotten the terrible scene of the night before, but Margie hadn't and neither had I.

Then it was time to go. As we got on our wraps I watched Margie bundle both girls into their pink winter coats, the white fur on the collars framing their tiny cherub faces. Normally I would have been bursting with pride about how cute they looked, but I was still carrying a huge leaden lump of anger that made every move difficult. I turned and almost tripped over the box Tina had wrapped in the gold paper. Irritably, I kicked it toward the living room and the Christmas tree, not wanting to be reminded of the trouble it had caused. But Tina darted in, picked up the box, and ran back to hand it to me. The beautiful gold wrapping paper was crumpled and creased and torn in one corner. Plastic tape was plastered all over it, but although it looked marred, my wee daughter gently held out her gift to me with loving pride.

"Here, Daddy, it's for you," she whispered, her blue eyes thoughtful and full of apprehension.

I grabbed the box from her tiny hands and noticed that it seemed quite light for its size.

What can it be? I wondered. I shook it gently but could hear nothing rattle inside.

The lights from our Christmas tree made the rumpled gold paper sparkle in a rainbow of colors. Slowly I tried to open the box, but the Scotch tape just wouldn't give. The harder I tried to get it undone, the more frustrated I became. Glimpses of yesterday's horrible scene flashed across my mind. I felt guilt, sorrow—and anger. I wanted to apologize, but still, Margie and Tina had both been wrong. Margie had humiliated me, and kids simply have to learn to obey.

Finally, I impatiently ripped the box open, but when I looked inside, the same terrible anger boiled up in my chest. My neck and face became a prickly red. Doing my best to keep my temper, I turned to Tina and said sharply, "Christina! Don't you know you should put something in a box before you wrap it up as a gift?"

Tina didn't cower back. She just looked up at me with tears coming down her face. Again the voices in my mind whispered, *You're just like your old man . . . you beat your kids . . . you make them cry.*

But with seemingly no fear, only love, Tina said, "But, Daddy, I *did* put something in it. I blew kisses into it! It's full of love just for you!"

I stood there feeling a gut-wrenching shock go through my entire body. Then goose bumps started crawling all over me. The gold wrapping paper that still clung to most of the box was literally glowing with a strange and wonderful light. Even though Tina's golden box was empty, it was full. She had given me the gift that I needed most. In return for my anger and the painful slaps and abuse, she had given me a child's unconditional love.

My pride and anger melted right there in the hallway. I dropped to my knees, hugged Tina, and begged her forgiveness. I hugged Paula and Margie and begged their forgiveness as well, weeping uncontrollably. "I'm so ashamed. You deserve better than this. Why don't you leave me here at home and go down to the farm to see Grandma and Grandpa? I don't deserve any of you. You were right and I was wrong. It's my pride, my stupid pride. I'm so ashamed."

Margie smiled through her tears and the girls hugged me and kissed me. "Daddy, don't cry, we love you . . . Daddy, don't cry."

Tina said, "I'm sorry, Daddy, I'm so sorry."

"No, Tina, *I'm* sorry . . . Daddy's sick . . . Daddy's sick."

"Are you going to the hospital, Daddy?"

"No, but I'm going to go to the 'Healer.' "

The girls didn't understand, but Margie did. I held all of their hands in mine as we prayed together. I asked God to kill the enemy—my anger. I begged to be cured. I never wanted to lose my temper again—ever. I pleaded for healing because, outside of Jesus, nothing was more important. My family was my only world, and I wanted the enemy to die.

Margie knelt down beside me and said, "I forgive you. I'm to blame, too, because I've been upset and I've been nagging you. I helped cause all of this, but we love each other and I know God's going to help us."

I clutched the golden box to my chest and said, "I'm going to keep this always. This is the best Christmas present of all."

Margie held our little girls tight and corrected me gently, "No, Daddy, Baby Jesus is."

"You're right, oh, you're right, Margie," I said. Then I turned and smiled at Tina, adding, "But this is the best *Christmas* I've ever had, and we're going to have a lot more of them."

And I prayed it would be so. Only God could do it. He had brought me so far, from a horror-filled Christmas of long ago, through a life of crime, to himself. He had given me the most wonderful family a man could want. My heart overflowed with thanks for the love of my children, for my wife, and for a wisdom far greater than mine that showed me what Christmas and love are all about.

TWO
"I'LL NEVER CRY AGAIN!"

I was seven when I lost the two things most dear to me in my little world. It was a grey and snowy November day when "Dog" (the only name I ever had for him) was hit by a truck. He was only a puppy, and I had gotten him for my birthday just the month before. I had never seen death before. It was 1943 and I was living with my family at the corner of Devine and Russell in Sarnia, Ontario—down by the tracks, in the slums, with the garbage dump right across the street.

My friends and I were too young to realize how "bad" we had it living next to a dump. We didn't even notice the stench, and besides, the dump was a great playground that provided an endless number of "hideouts" for our games and mock battles.

World War II was going strong, and trains loaded with American soldiers would pass our house almost daily. The trains came out of Chicago, bound for New York City where the soldiers were to ship out. It was a more direct route to cross the border at Sarnia, go through Ontario, and recross at Buffalo, New York. We watched the soldiers go by, waving out of the windows of the train. Sometimes flatcars would go by, loaded with cannons and tanks. Those soldiers were our heroes, and we often played war among the mounds of garbage, shooting at imaginary "Japs" and "Jerrys" with sticks or whatever we could find for guns.

Our war games were all fun and make-believe, of course. When somebody was shot and killed, he got up and went home for supper when he heard his mom calling. Death wasn't real—it was just part of having fun with my friends—until that day when Dog ran out in the street. I actually heard the sickening thud as the truck ran him down. He lay there in the street, not moving. The truck rumbled on. The driver didn't even bother to slow down.

With tears streaming down my face, I picked up the already cold and stiffening body of my puppy and carried it to our porch. Somebody had told my older brother Leroy and he helped me find an orange crate for a coffin. We laid Dog in the crate, put some newspapers on top of him, and carried him across the street to a huge mound of garbage. Using only our bare hands, we pulled away the garbage and made a hole for the orange crate. Then we covered it over as best we could, the rapidly falling snow helping us finish the job. In a few minutes there wasn't a trace of Dog's grave—I'd forgotten to put up a marker.

I went home and cried for days over Dog. I'd look out at the mound of snow-covered garbage that was Dog's grave and wonder when the trucks would come to shove it into the incinerator about a block away. That incinerator never stopped burning. The trucks would come with loads of garbage and dump them, and eventually one truck equipped with a snow plow blade would shove the mounds of refuse into the flames.

"It's OK, LaVern."* one of my brothers would tell me. "You'll get a new dog when we move to a new house. We can afford it because Dad got the new job. Right after Christmas—you'll see!"

But even the thought of a new house, away from the railroad tracks and the garbage dump, didn't console me. In fact, I rather liked the tracks and the garbage—they were the only world I had known. One day I saw the big truck with the snow plow blade attack the mound that was Dog's grave. Soon it was gone, into the incinerator. I pictured Dog being burned up and I cried some more.

Brokenhearted as I was, I never cried around my father. He was a brusque, no-nonsense Scotsman; a hard worker, but an even harder drinker who never liked to hear his kids cry—especially his sons. My dad believed that crying was for women—men just didn't ever show tears.

---

*My given name was LaVern. I changed it to Paul at age twenty, soon after becoming a Christian.

My father's name was Albert, but he went by the nickname "Ab." He was a skilled mechanic and carpenter and could build or fix practically anything. My mother was Christina, but my father usually called her "Teeny." They were both pure-blood Scots who had come to Canada in 1936 when the Great Depression still ravaged most of the world.

Mom had been a seamstress and milliner in Edinburghshire, and as a young girl she had been the top Highland Fling and sword dancer in her village. She was part of the Barclay clan, and her first cousin, Charles Alexander Barclay, had been awarded Chief of Arms by the decree of the Lyons' Court in 1901.

The Barclays were from the village of Towie, as was the Powers family. My father, Albert Edward Powers, was Mother's third cousin, and as was done in those days, they married and formed their own clan, which had the family motto From the Cross to a Crown. Their sword motto was Fight or Die, and as it turned out, my family practiced their sword motto much more diligently than their family motto.

In 1917, Mom and Dad moved to Glasgow, where he began work as an apprentice engineer in the new automotive factory. Life went well for them throughout the twenties, but when the depression hit in 1929, money and jobs became scarce. They held on until 1936, when they decided to emigrate to Canada. After arriving by ship from Scotland, they settled in the Petrolia-Oil City area in western Ontario. Later they moved to Sarnia, just across the U.S. border from Port Huron, Michigan.

For awhile my father tried to work at the automobile factories in Detroit, some fifty miles south in Michigan. He would ride down with friends at the beginning of the week and stay in Detroit until the weekend before coming home. That didn't last, either, and our family, which numbered four boys and a girl, scrimped along with barely enough to eat, subsisting on the few dollars a week my mother could make as a seamstress in a millinery shop in Sarnia.

When I turned seven that fall, Kathleen, firstborn in our family, was fifteen. Jimmy, my oldest brother, was thirteen, and Leroy was eleven. Beneath me was Bobbie, who was three and still taking afternoon naps in a crib in Mom's bedroom.

Just before my seventh birthday, my father had gotten on at the Imperial Oil Company in Sarnia as a pipe fitter and joiner. He worked in the "crack and oil" department, which took the gummy crude, boiled it to a bubbly syrup, and finally turned it into gas.

A lean, muscular man who stood five-foot-eight, my father hardly was what you would call warm and loving, or even friendly. He had flat grey eyes that could stare right through you, and when he wasn't working he spent most of his time out in the garage, which was filled with cars in various states of being dismantled or rebuilt. He loved to work out there for hours at a time, swapping stories with his drinking buddies, and of course there was always a bottle handy.

My father was a heavy drinker, if not an alcoholic. He had a quick temper and was very argumentative and opinionated. One of his favorite targets for criticism was the government, which he believed was full of thieves and cheats. Anything you could do to stay one step ahead of the government was the right thing, as far as my dad was concerned.

Despite our poverty, life for me and my brothers and sister was not totally miserable during those first few years. Mom and I were very close because she had nursed me through rheumatic fever when I was two. She had spent long hours keeping me amused and would often ask, "Now then, don't you want to take a wee nap, Laddie?"

"I've got a better idea, Mum . . . I want to ride the 'horsie'!"

"Ride the horsie? Aw now, you couldn't last until Mum went to all the work of putting her hair into braids, could you?"

"Oh yes, I could!"

"All right, but it will take a few minutes. . . .

"There now, two fine braids, and I still say I'm glad I left it long—after all, what would we do for reins if I had it bobbed off?"

"Give me the reins, give me the reins!"

"Here you are, Laddie, and mind to drive carefully."

"Get up, horsie, get up, horsie . . . bouncer, bouncer!"

We played that game often, as my mom did all she could to make the years in bed easy for me. At last I was fitted with braces for my legs and sent off to school. A year later, I was finally able to walk without the braces.

My parents were both strict, and though I got my share of spankings, I was never beaten or badly abused during my first seven years. As for being poor, I was too young to know just how poor we really were. I thought living down by the dump and the railroad tracks was exciting—something always new and different to get into or play with. When Dad got his job with Imperial Oil early in the fall of 1942, just as I turned seven, our family had a big celebration, with lots of food and, of course, plenty of liquor. My parents were planning to move to a much nicer and bigger house over on Cameron Street, several blocks away from the dump and the railroad tracks, but all it meant to me was I'd be going to a different school.

Late in November, the Imperial Oil Company threw a big pre-Christmas party, and my mother and father attended. Mom had been joining Dad in his drinking, and by then she was practically an alcoholic herself, often having to "lie down" during the middle of the day because she was recovering from a hangover. Of course, they drank heavily at the company party that night while one of our aunts baby-sat all of us kids. When my parents got home well after midnight, they were both blind-staggering drunk. Dad staggered into the house and fell asleep on the bed, but Mom staggered into a snowbank by the driveway and fell asleep next to the car.

The next morning Aunt Willabelle went home and Kathleen made porridge for the rest of us children. No one bothered to check our parents' bedroom; we could hear Father snoring—and you did not disturb Father after he had been out drinking the night before.

Jimmy, one of my older brothers, left for school first and took his usual route down the driveway. He glanced at a snowbank and thought he saw what looked like a dog lying there. He went over for a closer look and found our mother curled up in her coat.

Jimmy shouted for help, and the rest of us dashed out to lift Mom to her feet. She was still drunk and coughing badly. We all worked to get her into the house—Jimmy and Leroy at her sides, Kathleen in front, and I in back, brushing the snow off her coat. We got her inside and onto the Chesterfield couch, where Kathleen got her coat off and wrapped some blankets around her.

Kathleen told the rest of us to go to school, while she stayed home to try to fix Mom some tea and porridge. All the while Mom kept coughing heavily, looking very hot and feverish. Dad was still sleeping when we left for school. When we came home for lunch, Kathleen said she thought Mom would be OK, but we could still hear her coughing. I took some tea in for her.

Over the next few days, Mom didn't get any better. In fact, she got worse, coughing up horrible-looking stuff into strips of old sheets cut up for "hankies." There was a bottle with some red medicine that sat by her bed, and she seemed to take it often. Aunt Jean, Mom's sister, came over to help care for her and so did Aunt Ina, Jean's twin.

The days dragged by. Dad would come home and just sit on the Chesterfield couch and drink, hardly speaking to any of us. Now and then he'd growl, "Get your studies done," but that was about all. Then he'd go in and talk to Mom for awhile. I believe they truly loved each other, and I know Dad felt guilty for having staggered into the house to fall asleep on the bed without noticing that Mom had fallen in the snowbank. As far as he was concerned, it was his fault she was so sick.

The doctor came every few days. He was our family doctor, because Canada's system of socialized medicine required every family, no matter how poor, to have a doctor. His suit and bow tie were black, and he wore little wire glasses that hung on his nose. Like all doctors, he carried a black bag. As he left he never said much to any of us children. He would just shake his head and remind us, "Keep her warm . . . plenty of fluids."

Early in December, Kathleen decided to take us all downtown to buy Christmas presents. Somehow, by collecting bottles and cans, I had saved up the incredible sum of five dollars, and it would be my first Christmas to actually buy presents for everyone in the family. We went down to the old five-and-dime on Christina Street in Sarnia. I took out my five one-dollar bills with the king's picture on them, old and crumpled, and bought a hockey puck for Bill and another one for Leroy. I got some comic books for Jimmy—*Captain Marvel* and *Plastic Man*—and I bought some little lead soldiers for my younger brother, Bobbie.

Then I bought a necklace for Kathleen and a package of Ogden's tobacco for my father. But I spent most of my money on a special vanity set for Mom. It had a hair brush, a comb, and a mirror, all covered with imitation mother-of-pearl and trimmed with imitation gold. Kathleen helped me wrap it. We tied it with a red ribbon, and I laboriously printed on a card, "To Mom, from your loving son, LaVern."

I couldn't wait for Christmas to come. I had gone to a real

store, where they actually let me touch things on the counter. And I paid for everything with money of my own. This was going to be the best Christmas ever!

Although he was worrying about Mom, Dad still tried to keep the Christmas spirit. He went across the tracks to a wooded area and came back with a little tree that we trimmed with paper decorations we had made at school and popcorn we strung at home. We all worked on the tree and tried to be happy as we looked forward to having Mom feel better.

December 22 came, the last day of school before Christmas vacation. Everyone else was still at school having Christmas parties, but our second grade party had let out early. I dashed home just a little after lunchtime. A bunch of kids from down the street were going to build a snow fort, and I wanted permission to leave the house and go help.

As I came in, I saw that Dad was already home, sitting on the couch with a bottle in his hand, as usual. The doctor's car was outside too. I dashed to Mom's bedroom and through the door saying, "Mum, can I . . . ?" The next thing I heard was Aunt Ina saying, *"Shhh."* I looked across the room and saw her, as well as the doctor, standing near Mom's bed.

The lamp on the table cast a warm glow on Mom's long, brown hair, which spread across the pillow. She turned her head to look at me. Her face was drawn and unsmiling as she tried to raise her hand off the bed, but all she could manage was, "LaVer . . . ," and then her hand went limp.

I stared at Mom, and Aunt Ina finally said, "Get along with ya, Lad." The doctor leaned over and pulled the blanket up over Mom's face. "She's dead," he said, and in the next few seconds horrible scenes flashed through my seven-year-old mind.

I could hear the truck and Dog's squeal as he was hit and killed. I remembered Leroy saying, "Everything's going to be all right . . . ." Then I could see us putting Dog in the garbage and the snow plow coming to shove Dog's grave into the incinerator. And I knew they were going to do the same thing to Mom!

I turned and ran from the room, dashing across the living room to my dad, who was dozing in a drunken stupor. I shook him and even pounded his chest with my little fists, sobbing, "Don't let them, don't let them do it . . . ." He looked up at me with those flat grey eyes, and the next thing I felt was his fist in my face!

His blow knocked me all the way across the room. I remember lying there with blood streaming from my nose and mouth. Then I felt his work boots kicking and stomping me as he shouted, "For cryin' out loud! Shut up, you stupid kid. Real men don't cry, babies cry!" He continued to kick me in the side, in the face, everywhere, always repeating his charge about babies crying while real men don't cry.

I looked up at him from the floor, and his face was contorted in the most horrifying, angry look imaginable. All the monsters in the few movies or picture books I had seen never looked any worse than my father did at that moment.

Then I heard my aunt shouting, "Stop it!" The doctor screamed, "For God's sake, man, you'll kill him!" That seemed to bring my father to his senses, and he stood there panting as the doctor said, "Go to your wife."

As the doctor tried to patch me up, I could hear Aunt Ina in the bedroom screaming and shouting at my father about what he had done to me. The doctor told me it was OK to cry, but I kept shaking my head and refusing to do so. I vowed to myself, *I won't cry anymore—I'll never cry again.*

An ambulance finally came from the Sarnia General Hospital, and Aunt Ina made Dad stay in the bedroom while they took Mother's body out on a stretcher. About then Kathleen got home and so did Leroy and Jimmy. They wanted to know what was going on, but all Aunt Ina would say was, "Mind your own business."

Kathleen started to cry and then became hysterical. She knew Mom had died, and when she saw me with blood all over, she just didn't know what could have happened. Then the doctor told the ambulance driver to take me away too. It hurt when they moved me, but I wouldn't cry. At the hospital they took me into one room and Mother's body into another. I spent several days in the hospital, being treated for a broken wrist, broken ribs, a badly swollen eye, lacerations, and several missing teeth. The only people who came to visit me were Aunt Ina and Aunt Jean. My father was "too busy" arranging for Mom's funeral, and I guess my brothers and sister weren't allowed to come.

I was lonely in the hospital, but I never cried. Most little boys would have cried themselves to sleep at night, but I had vowed to never cry again. When sorrow and fear surged in my little chest, I would bite my lip until I drew blood, forcing myself never to shed a tear.

I opened this chapter by saying that at age seven I lost the two dearest things in my little world. Actually, I lost one other very precious possession: my childhood. After my dad beat me, screaming, "Men don't cry, babies cry," I vowed I'd never cry again. For the next thirteen years, I kept that vow. My childhood days—the horsie rides on Mom's back, the lighthearted play oblivious to the wretched squalor of our neighborhood—were gone. In their place was a bitter little boy who became a "man" overnight and who would pay a terrible price.

THREE
From Bad
to Really Bad

My mother's funeral was held December 26, but I didn't go because I was still in the hospital. When I finally got back home on December 30, the Christmas tree was still standing in the living room. I stood there alone for a long time looking at the bright ornaments. My eye found one of my favorites, a little copper bell that made a tinkling sound. As I reached out to touch it, I saw some gifts still lying unopened at the foot of the tree. One of them was the vanity set—the comb, the brush, and the mirror—which I had carefully wrapped and addressed "To Mom, from your loving son, LaVern."

"Mum, oh, Mum," was all I could whisper. And then her words from long ago came rushing back, and I could hear her sweet voice: "There you are, Laddie, and so you want to ride the horsie? I'm glad I left my hair long—two fine braids—whatever would you do for reins if I had it bobbed off?"

I should have cried under those circumstances—any kid would have—but my father had beaten all the tears out of me. "For cryin' out loud . . . !" he had shouted as he had kicked me into a pulp. Well, "crying out loud" was something I would never do again—never in my entire life!

There was a lot of confusion right after Mom died. All five of us were boarded out to nearby relatives, and for awhile there was talk that different aunts and uncles would adopt us. But this never happened, and by the latter part of January we were all back with my father in the new house on Cameron Street.

That was when a gum-chewing woman with long, dark hair and glasses entered our lives. Betty was a "lady of the evening" my father ran into at a bar a few days after Mom died. At least fifteen years younger than my father, she moved into our house to "help out," bringing along two children of her own: Donna, about two and a half, and Tommy, who was only three months old. Later there was speculation that Dad could have been Tommy's father because it turned out he had known Betty earlier. The story went that they had met while both of them were working at Imperial Oil. At any rate, moving in with us didn't prevent Betty from practicing her chosen profession. She used one of the upstairs bedrooms, and we would sometimes see men coming and going.

Betty came from a rather prominent family who farmed near Sarnia. Rebellious and headstrong, she left the farm to work in a factory in the city, had one child (Donna) out of wedlock, and was pregnant with another (Tommy) when she returned home because she couldn't make it financially.

As I heard the story, she went to church with her parents and was taking Communion at the altar rail when the old Episcopalian priest asked her, "Is it all well between you and the Savior? Have you confessed your sins?"

Betty became so irate at that question that she slapped the Communion bread right out of the rector's hands and stomped up the aisle and out of the church forever. She brought a real hatred of the church and the Bible into our home and constantly ridiculed anything and everything Christian. Our family had not been churchgoers even when Mom was alive. She and Dad would go to a church wedding, or something like that, but that was the extent of it. When Betty moved in, she saw to it that our family had *nothing* to do with the church. When Salvation Army workers would come to the house asking for donations, Betty just swore at them and slammed the door in their faces.

While church wasn't part of our lives, school was. As soon as I was able, I returned to class, this time at Hannah Memorial, the school in our new neighborhood. Up until Mom's death I had loved school. My first grade teacher back at Johnston Memorial was Mrs. MacIntyre, the creator of the famous "Dick and Jane" books used to teach reading to thousands of children throughout North America. I remember having the toughest time spelling—and even saying—the word *bicycle*. Mrs. MacIntyre would try to get me to pronounce *bicycle* correctly, but I had a funny little Scottish burr and always mangled it.

Even so, I liked that school because I was learning to read. It was a "wonderland" for me—a place of adventure with *Robinson Crusoe,* pirates, and *Treasure Island.* I loved stories and fantasy, and after Mom died I started going regularly to the movies—especially Saturday morning matinees. They were a retreat where I could vicariously become any hero I wanted—Roy Rogers, Gene Autry, or Hopalong Cassidy, just to name a few of the cowboys who were kings in those days.

But when I switched to Hannah Memorial School after our move, things went sour. Since I was the "new kid on the block," I got picked on and got into fights going to school, on the school grounds, and coming home—everywhere. Someone would shout, "Here comes the scum from the slums," and that would be enough to set it off.

Once in the classroom, nobody wanted to sit by me because I constantly smelled of urine. (After my dad gave me that beating, I began wetting the bed frequently.) The other kids liked to tease me about Betty. They would shout, "We heard about your old lady . . . we know what your mother does . . . she sleeps with other men." The only way they could have known anything like that was through their parents, and I'm sure that's how they found out about Betty, hearing their parents talk at the dinner table.

It also didn't help me to have a name like LaVern. You may recall a song, popular in the seventies, that told of all the troubles faced by "A Boy Named Sue." Well, Sue didn't have anything on LaVern, and I was constantly goaded into fights. LaVern was a very popular girl's name at the time due to the Andrew sisters, Maxine, Patti, and LaVerne. And to cap it all off, two girls in my class had the name LaVerne!

For some reason, nobody in our family ever thought about shortening my name to Vern, and so the name LaVern was my constant burden. It was a red flag that waved constantly, forcing me to prove I was too tough to ever be called a girl. And it wouldn't have helped to use my middle name, because it was Aloysius!

The following August my father married Betty, ironically enough, in a church service. I'm sure it was strictly for convenience or possibly some tradition my father wanted to uphold.

Betty didn't like being married in a church, but she had to go along with it.

I turned eight that year in October, and that's when I started stealing, along with some other kids that I was running with at school. Although the kids from "better" homes despised me, I did manage to find my own group—poor kids like me who didn't wear nice clothes and who usually smelled kind of "different."

By then, Kathleen had left home to live out at Camlachie, a little town on the shore of Lake Huron about fifteen or twenty miles north of Sarnia. She stayed with different friends for awhile and would occasionally come home, but would always be gone again soon. She began sleeping around near the Army station at London, Ontario, about sixty-five miles east of Sarnia. She lived with different boyfriends and had at least three children out of wedlock. Whenever she had a child, she would bring him home and Betty would help her take care of him, but eventually Kathleen was off again and Betty was left to raise Kathleen's children.

I usually got saddled with doing the baby-sitting, not only for Donna and Tommy, Betty's children, but for David and Buddy, Kathleen's first two kids. Kathleen also had another child whose name I can't remember. I took care of him for a few months also, but he died of crib death, something that Betty tried to blame me for. Fortunately, not even my father would believe that one.

Of all the children, I grew to hate Tommy the most because he was sickly and became Betty's favorite, much as I had become my own mother's favorite when I had rheumatic fever. I had to be extra careful not to get Tommy fussed, but he was always crying and getting me in trouble. All this—plus all the rumors about who Tommy's real dad might be—made me hate him, but I never harmed Tommy or any of the other kids.

The reason I wound up with all those screaming brats and washing all those dirty diapers by myself was that my older brothers just weren't around. Jimmy, my oldest brother, had already left home and gone to live with a minister, after being arrested any number of times for petty theft. Jimmy later turned out pretty well, became a hair stylist, and got married.

Between Jimmy and me was Leroy. Although he was still living at home at the time, he had a job as an usher at the Odeon and Park Theatres in Sarnia, so he was never available for much baby-sitting. Leroy would often sneak me into the Park Theatre, otherwise I seldom would have been able to afford to see many movies, even at the 1940s price of twelve to fifteen cents. From time to time Leroy got in trouble with the law, too, and later the judge gave him an option—reform school or the Navy. Leroy joined the Navy and went on to a career in the Canadian Armed Forces.

My father's drinking only got worse, and he became more and more abusive. He would hardly talk to me—perhaps he felt guilty about the beating he had given me—and most of the time I was ignored unless I aroused Betty's wrath for some petty reason. With all those kids running around wailing and crying and dirtying themselves, she always seemed to find plenty of reasons, and later she added more! About a year after marrying my father, she gained weight, "lost her figure," and went out of "business." To pick up some extra money, she started a child-care service, and soon several more wailing brats were added to my work load.

For some reason, Betty loved little babies and tiny children, but she never loved me or ever said one word of appreciation for all my slave labor. Actually, she seemed to enjoy riding me and inflicting all the pain she could—psychological and physical. One night we had roasted chicken for dinner and I was so ravenous I reached for another piece without asking. The next thing I knew, my hand was practically pinned to the table by the carving knife.

"Who said you could have any more, you little . . . ?" Betty snarled as I howled with pain. But *I didn't cry!* Nothing could make me cry, especially with my father sitting three feet away. He didn't even seem to notice what was going on—he just kept smacking his lips over a big piece of chicken and reading the paper.

I went to the bathroom and wrapped my hand in toilet paper to stop the bleeding. Later I went to my room and lay on my bed, holding my wounded hand against my chest and thinking of what I'd like to do to Betty if I ever had the chance. The wound was deep, and to this day I carry a scar just behind my right index finger.

To get away from the madhouse called home, I started staying away more and more with my gang of friends from school. They actually became my "real family" of sorts. We'd meet at a park a few blocks from my house, over by the slides and swings, and then plan what we would do that day.

A kid named Bob was one of our leaders. He was older, around twelve, and was kind of crazy even then. He would swagger up to other guys with his hands in his back pockets and just sort of sway back and forth, chewing on a toothpick and staring with a strange look in his eyes. If anybody backed down, even the tiniest bit, he'd nail them. Bob was always talking out of the side of his mouth and chewing on that toothpick. His father was a fireman and he used to smack Bob on the side of the head and say, "You're going to swallow that thing and choke yourself."

Before he had turned twelve, Bob had seen his father crushed when he jumped off the back of a fire truck as it was backing up. Bob stood right there and watched his dad die. He was already in the gang by then, and so was his older brother—a boy about fifteen. Several older guys also hung around from time to time, but basically our core group was a bunch of us who ranged from eight to twelve years old. We were drawn together by a mutual need for some kind of friendship and affection, which we weren't getting at home. My special buddy was Jimmy D, who was about my age.

All in all, there were twenty-two guys in our gang. Of the twenty-two, only eight lived beyond the age of thirty. Bob later went insane in a mental institution and killed himself. Most of the others also met violent deaths, usually after overdrinking.

When I joined the gang, they hadn't been into doing much actual stealing—yet. We started by shoplifting chocolate bars, Lifesavers, and cigarettes. It was all part of a street game we played called "Who Dots the *I?*" One guy would cover his eyes, and then the rest of us would draw a circle on his back with our fingers as he leaned against a tree. And then we'd repeat the little rhyme, "I draw the circle, I cut the pie, I draw the question mark, who dots the *I?*"

The guy who was "it" had to turn around and guess who dotted the *I.* If he got it right, the guy he chose had to take his turn at the tree. But if he got it wrong, the rest of us could dare him, or double-dare him, to do all kinds of things—take his bicycle and go over a wooden ramp, or maybe climb an extra-high tree, or maybe grab something at Campbell's store, the Berry Box, or Walpole Drugs.

But after awhile, we didn't need "Who Dots the *I?*" as an excuse for pilfering. We just planned to grab things, and we all took our share. We all loved the movies and would go on Saturday mornings to different theatres in downtown Sarnia. In a way, the movies became our crime school, and we got all kinds of different ideas about how to rip things off and not get caught by the cops.

Soon we had a little system working, and we'd go into a store like Campbells, or the Berry Box—a "hamburger and French fries" kind of place—and ask the attendant for something that we knew was in the back room. While she went out back, we'd fill our pockets with everything we could grab and then beat it. We loved hanging out around the Berry Box. It had a jukebox, and I can remember playing some of my favorite songs over and over: "Cruising Down the River," "How Much Is That Doggie in the Window?" and "Wheel of Fortune."

I got my nickels and dimes for the jukebox and going to the movies by selling occasional pop bottles I'd find, or by ripping off milk money people would leave on the back stoop in the empty bottles for the milkman. Later, burglary and other forms of theft kept me in plenty of spending money.

Eventually, of course, the stores became wise to us, and when we came in we'd get chased out because they knew what we were after. It was then that we started breaking into homes, and once we broke into Campbell's store at night and stole several cartons of cigarettes and candy bars.

Bob, our leader, seemed to know when "So-and-so is away— they're gone on holiday." I can remember one of the first houses we ever burglarized. We were all scared stiff, but when you're part of it, you just can't back out. About five of us slipped up on the back veranda, opened a back window, and boosted Raymond, one of the smaller kids, through the opening. Then Raymond let us in the kitchen door.

It was the home of an elderly couple who had been nice to us and given us cookies a few days before. We made a beeline to the cookie jar and stole the rest of the cookies, then we went to the bedroom and rifled the drawers to find money. We didn't find much money, but we did take some dirty comic books, little eight-page novels featuring heroes like Ally Oop and Popeye, doing things no one ever saw in any legitimate cartoon or comic book. It was the beginning of our sex education. We also stole some money and some brandy in a beautiful decanter. It was then I got my first drink of hard liquor. It burned like fire all the way down.

It was about that time that we started learning to smoke as well as drink. At first we would cough our heads off, but we soon got on to it and became expert in inhaling a big drag and blowing it through our noses.

We did most of our mischief in the spring and summer because it was too cold to do much in the winter. After being cooped up all winter, we'd get out and start to drive everyone in the neighborhood a little crazy. We liked playing ball out in the street, and neighbors were always calling the police because they were afraid we would break a window. And whenever we did rip off someone's house, they would tell the police we had done it, but of course there was no proof.

The police would come to the house and demand, "Did you do this?" My father or Kathleen or Jimmy would protect me by saying, "Can you prove it? Who saw them go in there?" After the police left, my father would turn on me and say, "What did you do that for?" He might cuff me, smack me, or kick me. If the police were especially hard to convince, he'd take me downstairs, strip off all my clothes and beat me with an old rubber hose he'd unhook from the wringer washing machine. That hose really hurt, and my father usually whacked me with it anywhere from ten to twenty times before he'd quit. But I was too tough to cry! I had settled that back when I was seven, on the day Mom died. I knew I would never cry again.

I started drinking more and more of the liquor we'd steal from homes and stores. Sometimes I'd be gone from home for two to three days at a time because I was so drunk. When I finally did sneak into the house through a cellar window, or through an upstairs window over the front veranda, my father would find me and take me downstairs and beat me some more with that rubber hose. At times the beatings were so severe that I had to stay home from school, but I didn't change—I only got worse, as did my brothers and sister. Jimmy, Leroy, and even Kathleen all got their share of beatings with that hose, and later on my little brother, Bobbie, took his turn.

Eventually our gang started crossing the St. Clair River, going from Sarnia over to Port Huron, Michigan, in the United States. We would steal a rowboat and row across, usually stopping at Stag Island, about halfway over. A settlement of Indians lived there, and we became acquainted with a lot of the Indian kids, who would provide places where we would temporarily stash our loot. Sometimes they went along to help us with our thievery. They became our good friends, and we often shared stolen cigarettes and booze with them.

In Port Huron we continued our crime spree, burglarizing homes and robbing gas stations. Actually, we didn't rob the stations themselves. Our favorite target was the cigarette machine, located in the front of the station and almost always left unprotected. We'd wait until late at night, then pry the machine open and claim a double prize—the money as well as the cigarettes. These we would take back across the river to Sarnia and sell to workers in the Imperial Oil Refinery and other factories nearby. We gave the workers a good deal—ten packs for a dollar. They knew they were stolen, but they never asked us any questions.

From Port Huron we eventually moved south to Detroit, hitchhiking or stealing bicycles to get down there where, again, we'd burglarize homes or rip off cigarette machines. We picked homes that were all dark and counted on no one being home, but sometimes they were and we'd have to run like crazy. We had several close calls, but we never got caught—at least not in Detroit.

Once I stole a lady's purse from a radio station in Sarnia. I was just hanging around in the waiting room, and the receptionist had gone to another room for a minute. I spotted the purse, grabbed it, and ran. It had over two hundred dollars in it, and I found a couple of friends to help me celebrate. We caught the ferry over to Port Huron and pigged out on all kinds of junk food. Then we bought cylinder-type Western guns—toy guns, to be sure—but they looked real to us and made us feel as if we were big and tough.

Later, however, the police came to my door and took me downtown for stealing that purse. Somebody had identified me, and I had to go before a juvenile judge in Sarnia. He gave me a stern lecture and then remanded me to the custody of my parents.

Coming before the judge happened frequently for me. On one occasion I was arrested for being part of a group who had gotten rowdy and broken a lot of store windows on a downtown Sarnia street. Another time I was nailed for stealing bicycles, and once I was picked up while coming home from the movies late at night—for breaking curfew.

Every time, however, I was only lectured, maybe threatened with reform school, and then sent home with my parents.

One thing none of us ever tried was grabbing a woman's purse off her shoulder and running. In those days the purses usually had big straps, often made of leather, and it was just too hard to get them away from the women who carried them. Besides, we'd go to the movies and watch the Dead End Kids and the Bowery Boys, and every time they tried snatching purses they got caught.

As I said, we learned a lot from the movies. We'd see Jimmy Cagney get sent to the Big House and hear the police telling him, "It was that big bill you put out that led us to you." So, when we stole money from cigarette machines or when we burglarized money from homes, we'd change big bills into smaller ones and smaller bills into coins. It wasn't hard to do—we'd go into a restaurant or a store and say, "Can you please change this? My dad needs to use the phone," or, "My mom needs change for the coin laundry."

We kept all of the money in Jimmy D's garage in a special hiding place. The garage was all boarded up, and to get in you had to shinny up a tree, inch your way along a limb, and then drop through a window in the back. That was where we'd go to stash our loot, look at dirty comic books, and learn the latest techniques for breaking and entering from older guys who knew more about it.

Whenever we needed money to go to the movies or buy candy or whatever, we'd pay a visit to Jimmy D's garage. We agreed to take only enough for what we needed and no more. That way we were never seen spending large amounts of money, and if the police did stop and question us, we never had a lot of money in our pockets and they couldn't pin anything on us. Naturally, somebody was always taking a little more than his share from the money cache, and we were always arguing and fighting among ourselves over who took all the cash.

By the time I was ten, I'd gotten into so much trouble at school and with the law that my father was ordered to take me to a psychologist at the Sarnia General Hospital because I was "emotionally disturbed." I had to sit there and answer questions with my father listening—questions such as, "Why do you hate your father?"

I couldn't tell the psychologist how he pounded on me and whipped me with a big rubber hose, and he probably wouldn't have believed me anyway. All I would say was, "I don't know . . . I don't know." Then the psychologist got a brilliant idea and asked, "Were you jealous of your younger brother, Bobby? And what about all the other little children that you have to care for and take care of?"

"Yeah, that's it," I admitted. I decided to go along with him, and besides, he wasn't far off. Changing all those diapers and being forced to baby-sit for all those screaming kids was definitely part of what I had to deal with.

All the while my dad sat there and watched me with those flat grey eyes with the yellow tinges. I could never look him, or anyone else, in the eye, except maybe my gang buddies. My self-esteem was in shambles throughout my childhood and teenage years.

Those visits to the psychologist didn't accomplish a thing. I kept playing hooky from school, running with my gang, stealing—and drinking. When I was eleven, a teacher at my school found me drunk and reported me to the Children's Aid Society. I was sent to see another psychologist at St. Joseph's Hospital to be counseled for alcoholism. Betty or occasionally Kathleen would take me on those trips.

Nothing helped. In June of the year I was twelve, I was gone from home for a couple of weeks, sleeping under bridges, in shacks, in hobo camps, in cardboard cartons in the back of stores—anywhere. During that time I robbed a taxi stand, a small building that dispatched the cabs by radio. Cabbies would bring their cash to the stand and leave it in a drawer, and I hung around and watched to learn the patterns of the cab dispatcher. One day when he went out back for a nature call and nobody else was around, I was waiting behind one of the cabs. I darted in, grabbed the money out of the drawer, and shot out of there. That time I got over a hundred dollars.

One night I broke into a home, and as I filled a sack with different items, I found a loaded .22 pistol in a drawer. I decided to take it along—I had never had a real gun before. What I didn't understand was that now I had the potential to be more than a thief and a burglar. It didn't take long for that gun to change my life forever.

FOUR
FROM REALLY BAD TO REFORM SCHOOL

"You little . . . get your hands out of my purse! I'll kill you, you no good little thief!"

Brandishing her cane, the old carnival lady started across her tent, ready to brain me if she could. I had her money—about five hundred dollars—in one hand and the gun I had stolen earlier in the other. Raymond, who had come along to help, cowered in the corner whimpering, "We didn't mean nothin'. . . ." Jimmy D was outside somewhere, supposedly being a lookout, but he hadn't done very well. The old lady had us cold.

"Get away from me, you old biddy, or I'll blow your stupid head off." I tried to sound tough, but she could see my hand shaking. She just laughed and kept coming, waving her cane and uttering curses I'd never heard before, not even from my father.

"You won't do anything, you little . . ." The next moves seemed to happen in slow motion. It wasn't supposed to happen, but it did. We had been planning to rob the old lady for weeks after spotting her flashing a roll of bills at the Brigden Fairs, about twenty miles from Sarnia. As we strolled by a hamburger stand, we heard someone ask her what she was going to do with "all that money." She grunted and said, "I'm going to keep it, what else? We're going to move on anyway, and I've got it all right here in my purse."

She was an older lady, a real hardcase "carny" type who ran one of the concessions where they hustled cupie dolls. We could see she had a big roll of bills. We tried to figure out a way to con her out of it then and there, but as we tried to build up our courage, all we managed to do was get drunk, and then it was too late.

A few days later we followed the carnival back to Sarnia. Then we watched and waited our chance while sitting under a bridge drinking beer. I had tried out the pistol I had stolen by shooting at some trees in the woods. I brandished it to impress my buddies and said, "Don't worry. If the old lady gets in the way, I'll scare the pantaloons right off of her."

One morning nothing much was happening because the carnival didn't open until afternoon. Jimmy D, Raymond, and I decided to go ahead with it. When we saw the old lady leave her tent, we moved in, leaving Jimmy D outside as lookout in case the old lady came back. Once inside, it was easy to find her cash box, which wasn't even locked. I had it open in a flash. Inside were tickets and a purse with the money. I had just grabbed the money when the old lady completely surprised us. She had come back to the tent from another direction, and Jimmy D hadn't even seen her!

Now we were caught, cornered with no way out, and she was almost on top of us! I was scared out of my wits, and without realizing it I pulled the trigger twice. She took both bullets in the side. She slumped over, but I didn't think I had hurt her very badly. We jumped past her and got out of there as fast as we could.

Jimmy D and Raymond were white with fear. We could hear screaming and shouting behind us as we dashed across the railroad tracks and into the woods. We made it to an Esso service station, ducked into the restroom, locked the door, and divided the take. As we split up, I told Jimmy D and Raymond, "I scared the old dame, but I didn't hurt her bad. She's fat . . . I didn't hurt her too bad . . . now let's get out of here!"

The last I saw of Jimmy D and Raymond, they were hustling back toward Sarnia. I headed east toward Highway 402. My plan was to hitch a ride to London and then on to Toronto where I could lose myself in the big city. We'd gotten about five hundred dollars out of the old lady's purse. I'd given Jimmy D and Raymond most of the small bills, about a hundred dollars, and I took everything else. I stuffed my share of the money in my shirt and kept moving fast. The gun wasn't weighing me down;

I'd thrown it in the river as we ran from the carnival area.

I decided I should try to hide for awhile in Petrolia, a few miles to the east, but I lucked out by hitching a ride with a trucker at a gas station. I told him I needed a ride to go in to see my father in London . . . that I was living with my mother in Sarnia, but my father lived in London and I needed to see him. As I got into the truck, the driver said, "What's the matter, kid, you seem nervous."

I looked at him and shrugged, "I guess I'm just scared of people."

It was about an hour's drive to London, about halfway to Toronto. He let me out near the army barracks because I said my father was there. I found a kid wearing a jacket about my size, and I bought it off of him for a few dollars. That way I could get rid of my jacket and not look like the guy the police would now be looking for.

I headed into town and got something to eat. Then I went down to the train station and found out a train was leaving in twenty minutes for Toronto. I had never been to Toronto. For that matter, I'd never bought a train ticket. I went up to the ticket window and told the man, "I need a ticket to Toronto on the next train. I'm supposed to get off downtown to meet my aunt."

He said, "That would be Union Station, Sonny. You sure you'll know your aunt when you see her?"

"Yeah, I stay with her every now and then, and this time she's going to take me to the Canadian National Exhibition."

"Oh!" said the ticket seller. "You'll have a grand time . . . that's really a big thing."

I paid for my ticket with small bills, keeping the twenties and fifties in my jacket pocket. I scampered for the train and found a seat. As soon as it got rolling, I went to the restroom and transferred a lot of the money to my shoes for safer keeping.

When the conductor came by to collect tickets, he gave me a hard look, but I fed him the same story about my aunt and going to the Canadian National Exhibition. He seemed to buy it, and when the train stopped in the Union Station in Toronto, I was the first one off—and into the crowd in a flash.

That train ride began three weeks of living on the run, sleeping where I could, usually in all-night theatres. I loved movies anyway, and once inside I could buy all the hot dogs and popcorn I wanted, which usually made me sick. In the daytime I wandered the city, stealing clothes off clotheslines and trying to stay out of the way of anything with a uniform. It was getting near time for kids like me to be back in school, and I didn't want them to pick me up as a truant.

One day I walked by a newsstand and saw a headline in the *Toronto Star*: "Woman Dies after Carnival Shooting." I bought a paper and read the story. It told all about the robbery and how the woman had died later of "complications." Her assailants were described as local boys, probably in their early teens. Police were investigating, but no arrests had been made. Now I was really scared. I was a murderer—one life exchanged for five hundred bucks.

My stomach was constantly churning and burning inside. Doctors would later tell me that I had ulcers, but I didn't know it then. All I knew was I had to keep on the move, worried about every shadow and absolutely petrified by any kind of uniform. I stopped going to two of the theatres in Toronto because the ushers wore uniforms with caps. When these guys came down the aisle, I thought they were the police, and I would have to slip out to the bathroom and throw up. Most of the time I was terrified and shaky, but I wouldn't cry.

One night I came out of a movie theatre and two punks grabbed me and beat me up. They took the few dollars I had in my pockets, but they missed the rest of the money, which was in my shoes. I decided it was time to get out of Toronto and get back to Sarnia before trying to slip into the United States and hide out somewhere—Chicago maybe. I had just enough money left for a train ticket to Sarnia, and once I got there I headed downtown to contact Jimmy, a bootblack I used to work with sometimes on Front Street shining shoes.

I found Jimmy at the usual pool hall, which had some shoeshine chairs in the back. I slipped up to him and tried to look casual as I asked him to loan me some money because I was broke. My share of the five hundred was gone, and I had nothing. Jimmy gave me a funny look and said he would see what he could do. "You want to set up a box?" he asked, wondering if I wanted to make a few bucks shining shoes.

"No," I replied, not bothering to tell him that the last place I wanted to be was in a pool room on Front Street, shining shoes in plain sight for any cop to see. "When do you want me to come back?"

"I'll meet you right here in a couple of hours," Jimmy said. It was around nine o'clock when I left the pool hall. I killed the next two hours hanging around side streets and alleys, always wary of police cars or any kind of uniform.

At exactly 11:00 P.M. I was back at the pool hall to meet Jimmy. I saw him back by his shoeshine chair and started toward him when suddenly two policemen were right behind me! I never even saw them coming. One grabbed me by the shoulder and snarled, "You're LaVern Powers . . . we've been looking for you, you little punk." He pushed me up against the wall of the pool hall while my "buddy" Jimmy scooted off. The fink had set me up with a phone call to the police, letting them know where and when they could find me.

The other cop grabbed my arm and twisted it behind my back as he growled, "Like to shoot people, do ya?" They slapped handcuffs on me, and by that time a police car had rolled up. They just opened the back door, shoved me in, and I flopped across the seat.

They took me straight to the police station. I was put in a holding cell, which had no other occupants that night. Early the next morning, a policeman came in and asked very officially, "Your name is LaVern Powers?"

Rubbing the sleep from my eyes, I answered, "Yes."

"You're being charged as a juvenile for taking the life of . . ." He read the carny lady's name, a name that I've long since forgotten. "Do you agree with this?"

"I don't know . . ." was all I could manage.

"You stupid little . . . you have no idea what you've done, do you?" He stomped out, slamming the cell door behind him.

That afternoon I was transferred from the police station to the Sarnia City Jail on Christina Street, across from the Catholic church and school. They gave me a cell to myself, and it was my home for the next twenty-eight days.

I remember looking out the bars through a window and seeing the Catholic church tower across the street. Years later I would be in that same building, looking out that same window. But then it would be a hotel, and I would be there for vastly different reasons. Now I was in jail, being held like any adult because Sarnia had no juvenile hall. On the other side of the jail were drunks in holding tanks and people who had been arrested for all kinds of crimes. They kept me alone in one of three cell

units, under what they called "psychiatric observation," until
they could figure out what to do with me.

There were comic books in the cell, and I passed the hours
with Superman, Captain Marvel, Mickey Mouse, Batman, the
Green Lantern, and other fantasy characters. I wasn't a good
reader, but I loved comic books because they had lots of pictures and simple words.

As the days passed, I sat there thinking, *It's over . . . what are
they going to do with me? But at least I don't have to go home
and face all those brats and all those dirty diapers. Now they'll
just put me away somewhere.*

I'd heard a lot about reform schools from older guys, and I'd
even seen some movies about them. I wasn't scared. In fact, I
sort of looked forward to reform school. No jailer could be
worse than Betty or my father.

As the days went by in the Sarnia jail, one of the guards gave
me a book. It was all about how to do magic tricks and illusions,
written by some guy named William Dexter. Fortunately I didn't
have to read a lot because it had lots of pictures showing how to
do card and coin tricks. I begged a pack of cards off of somebody and practiced, and by the time they were ready to transfer
me out of the Sarnia jail, I already knew several of the tricks.

My hearing was in juvenile court in an old gray brick building
on Christina Street. The only person there from my family was
my stepmother, Betty. My father was working, and none of the
younger kids in the family were allowed to come. I doubt they
would have wanted to anyway.

I was led into the room, and the judge read the charges
against me: armed robbery and attempted murder. For some
reason I never understood, the law didn't choose to charge me
with the old carny lady's actual murder. She had died of "complications" following the shooting.

The judge peered down from his bench and said, "LaVern
Powers, we've had you here before. In fact, you've been a
constant visitor in this room."

I made some kind of smart retort, and the judge snapped,
"Stand up and get that smirk off your face. With all the evidence,
plus your own confession to the crime, it is the judgment of this
court that you be sent to the Bowmanville Training School for
Boys to be held under observation for an indefinite period of
time. And that until such time as you leave for Bowmanville,

you'll be held under observation here in the Sarnia jail."

I looked over at Betty. She just smiled grimly, nodding her head in agreement with the judge. She was glad to get rid of me, and frankly, the feeling was mutual. Again I thought of all those diapers I wouldn't have to change, and I almost looked forward to Bowmanville. Over the next two weeks, the court psychiatrist kept dropping by my cell at least twice a week to ask me the typical questions: "How did I like it at home? What did I think of my father? My mother? My brothers and sisters? Did I like people?"

I always answered with smart remarks and an I-don't-care attitude. I wasn't sure what the psychiatrist put on his report, but I'm sure it wasn't anything like "normal."

At the end of twenty-eight days, I was told I was leaving the Sarnia jail, and so I packed my "suitcase"—a paper sack that I filled with a few pieces of clothing, some comic books, and my book of magic tricks. The comics and the magic book weren't mine, of course, but I decided I could make better use of them than the guy who would use the cell next, so I took them along.

I was handcuffed to a policeman for the train ride, which didn't take me to Bowmanville but to another facility at Cobourg, a town about fifty miles east of Toronto on the shores of Lake Ontario. Because I was still under thirteen, the judge decided to switch me into Cobourg, which handles boys that age. Bowmanville was for boys thirteen to fifteen, and with my birthday coming up, I would be transferred later.

Cobourg was a minimum-security place, with no fences, barbed wire, or bars on the windows. It looked like a big private school, and after I was registered they sent me to a room in what they called "the holding reception area." Later I was supposed to be transferred into one of several little cabins out behind the main building.

Three other guys had arrived with me, and as we sat locked in our room we started making plans about how to get out of there. One of the guys had found a nail file somewhere, and with it he unscrewed the big brass doorknobs from the bathroom door and from the inside of the room's main door. When the doorknobs were put in a pillowcase, they became a deadly weapon, far more lethal than any blackjack. I was assigned the job of clobbering Mr. Woods, our guard, when he came in to check us for the night. Then we would make a break for it!

About an hour later we heard him coming down the hall. His key turned in the lock, and he walked into the room, not suspecting a thing. I was lurking on a top bunk right by the door, and he never saw me swing the pillowcase full of doorknobs. They caught him with a sickening crunch right on top of the head, and he went down without a sound. We grabbed his keys and left him lying there as a pool of blood started to spread across the floor.

We dashed down the hall to the front door, and it seemed to take forever to find the right key and get it open. Then we were down the steps and racing across the large lawn in front of the building. Cobourg had no fences, and all I could think of as we ran for the street was, *I'm free ... this time they'll never be able to catch me again!*

FIVE
DOING HARD TIME
IN THE DIGGER

We headed across the lawn as fast as we could run, but we
never even got a hundred yards away. The commotion had
alerted the other guards, and they were after us in an instant.
They caught up to us at the edge of the grounds, tackled us, and
slapped us around. Two of them really manhandled us with
body punches, karate chops, and elbows placed in just the right
spot.

They dragged us back inside, where we learned that Mr.
Woods was hurt pretty bad. Although he would recover and be
able to continue working as a guard, Mr. Woods would be
partially paralyzed for the rest of his life.

"You're at it again, you little killer!" one of the guards
screamed at me. "I'd like to put you out of your misery!"

All the while I was screaming, shouting, swearing, kicking at
them, telling them I hated them, and I wanted them to drop
dead. "Go ahead, kill me! *Who wants this?*"

The next day I was taken to see the shrink, and we went over
the usual business about all my hostility. I just glared at him
every now and then, saying, "Yeah . . . I guess so. . . ."

In less than two weeks I was out of Cobourg and on my way
to Bowmanville, a bigger, more secure facility located a few
miles west near Oshawa. During the war it had been a prisoner-
of-war camp for captured German soldiers. I was told it was a
big place, surrounded by barbed wire.

Two guards took me to Bowmanville by car. I had a belt
around my stomach with a chain through it attached to my feet

and hands. One guard drove the car and the other sat in the backseat with me, watching my every move. We drove up to the gate, and I could see the twelve-foot fence with barbed wire on top. As the gate swung open, one of them said, "Here you are, Powers. Before we're through, we'll break you . . . you can bet on it."

I guess he expected me to cry—I was still only twelve—but I used the defense that had always worked best, even when my father was beating me: no tears, just a blank stare. Then a little smirk crossed my lips, and when he saw that, the guard really got angry. "You smart little punk. We'll wipe that smirk off your face and stuff it down your throat. We're going to break you, Powers . . . you're finished!"

They took me inside to a reception holding area much like the one at Cobourg. I was given the brownish orange khaki pants and shirt that identified me as a new inmate, and then I went through a battery of tests and exams. I spent several days in the reception holding area, getting a medical checkup and being tested to see where I was on the educational ladder and what my natural gifts or skills might be.

With all the school I'd skipped, it was no surprise that I scored low on things like reading and math, but I got high marks on manual dexterity. I wound up mostly in manual arts classes. They did try to teach me basic reading and arithmetic, but I did so poorly the teachers gave me up as a lost cause.

I learned that Bowmanville was divided into several kinds of barracks, or "houses," which held inmates of different levels of ability. Center House was considered maximum security for the really tough older guys. South House was for the above average who did well in the typical school subjects such as math and English. North House was for the below average, manual arts types. Kiwanis House, donated to the Province of Ontario by the Kiwanis Club, was for truly gifted kids. And Jury House was for the runts—the little kids who needed to be kept away from the older, bigger guys.

I was good-sized for my age. My tests put me in the manual arts category, so I was assigned to North House and marched over to my new quarters. I soon learned that you marched everywhere in Bowmanville—most of the guards had military backgrounds, and they always made us step to it. They wore grey slacks, white shirts, red ties, and blue blazers with the

Ontario government crest on the pocket. Their official title was house master, but they were *guards,* believe me.

North House was like all the other barracks—a long one-story building with high walls that gave the impression of two stories. The buildings had been built with such high walls for a reason. That's where they put the windows, high above so the inmates couldn't get at them. And besides, they had bars. The place had definitely been a prisoner-of-war camp, and now I too was a prisoner, waging my own private war against the world.

I went inside North House and found myself in the locker room. Each of the fifty inmates had his own small wooden locker with a padlock, as well as some shelves on which he could keep other items that he didn't want to lock up. To the left of the locker room was the bathroom, which had toilets and urinals on one side and showers and sinks on the other. Dividing these two areas was a broom closet where they kept floor polishers, wax, and other things for keeping the place clean. Through another door was the lounge, a large room with a pool table, piano, tables, and magazines. This was the place to sit and relax—when you had some spare time.

To the right of the locker room was the house master's room, and next to that was a goods and equipment room holding clothing and other needed supplies. Behind the goods and equipment room, in a far corner of the building, was a small room about the size of a large closet. It had no windows or lights, only an air vent at the bottom of the door. Inside were "a cot and a pot," and that was all. This was the infamous Digger, Bowmanville's version of solitary confinement.

I would get acquainted with the Digger in short order. In fact, it only took a couple of days before someone got wind of my name and decided to see if I had any more guts than a girl. I proved I had the guts, but for fighting I got tossed in the Digger for an entire day.

Discipline was always firm and swift at Bowmanville. We lived by the clock and moved with military precision from place to place—"hup, hup, hup, hup." Reveille was at six-thirty, and we had to be up, showered and dressed and ready to march to the dining hall by seven. If anybody diddled or tried to catch an extra ten minutes of sleep, he was usually in for a rough day, starting with a swift kick or jab from one of the rougher guards, who actually were nicely dressed thugs.

Or the jab or kick might come from one of the "red ties," the inmates who were just about ready to get out on probation. They were the equivalent of trustees, as far as the guards were concerned. To get in a scrap with a "red tie" was pointless because you always lost. It was his word over yours every time.

The color of your tie identified where you were in Bowmanville's rehabilitation program. New inmates got a blue tie, which said you needed constant supervision and had few or no privileges. After awhile you could work your way up to a green tie, which gave you a few more privileges and maybe the chance to earn trust by doing simple things like delivering messages. "Red ties" could go into town on a pass or work at nearby farms to earn extra money. Of course, they always lorded it over everyone else.

If a kick or a jab wasn't enough to get you going, the guards might assign extra kitchen duty or a job polishing the floors in your own barracks. Or they might decide to make you "duck walk" up and down the compound outside the barracks buildings. If you gave them any lip, they'd keep you duck walking—in any kind of weather—until your legs turned to putty.

After showering and getting dressed, we would line up outside our barracks and then march over to the dining hall. We had to be there by seven because we only had thirty minutes to eat breakfast, which was usually some kind of porridge, oatmeal, watered-down stew, or soggy toast. With three hundred guys to feed, the cooks weren't too worried about how "crisp and golden brown" our toast was. It usually came out cold and limp. For "butter" they used some sort of melted margarine, slopped on with a paint brush.

We would often have prunes for fruit. Some occasional brown sugar on our oatmeal was considered a luxury. Although Bowmanville had its own herd of dairy cows, our milk was still watered down so that it would go farther.

After breakfast most of us were marched to the main rec hall for an assembly or, on other days, straight to classes. Each day two or three guys from each barracks were sent back to clean and mop their house—we all had to take our turn at that.

Class assignments depended on your level. If you were considered above average or "bright," you might go to math, English, geography, or history class. If you didn't show much promise there, you got sent to sheet metal, woodwork, or leather working. Gym class with formal P.E. activities came at least one hour a day. Classes lasted until the noon march back to the dining hall for lunch, which might include hot dogs or liver. Vegetables depended on what the farm had been growing: in the summer we had plenty of fresh tomatoes, lettuce, turnips, and cabbage.

After lunch came rest period, when those who smoked could "roll their own" with "makin's" provided by the guards. The tobacco was strong and the roll-your-own cigarettes tasted terrible, but they were better than not smoking at all. Smokers were limited to only three cigarettes a day. Guys who didn't smoke were known as being "on the tuck," and for their special treat they would get a chocolate bar or a Coke once a week.

If you fouled up, your privileges were gone for the day, maybe two or three days, or even longer—no smokes, no candy, nothing. For a chain smoker like me, to lose smoking privileges even for a day was tough, so I usually stayed in line unless somebody pressed my button—which happened all too often. All the psychologists who examined me had put "full of hostility" on my reports, and they were right. I hated the world and everybody in it. One of my favorite mottos was "All people should drop dead!"

After rest period it was back to class or to shop until late afternoon. And then it was "march to your barracks," where you cleaned up and got ready for supper at six. And, of course, at six you *marched* over to the dining hall and had supper, which was usually not much better than breakfast or lunch: potatoes, spaghetti, sometimes greasy pork chops or stringy roast beef.

We never ate any steak, but we did have turkey on Thanksgiving and Christmas. Pork 'n' beans was a highlight, and we often had toasted cheese sandwiches. For dessert we usually got some kind of pudding, Jell-O, or stale cookies.

Everyone pulled regular kitchen duty. You could choose either to help prepare the meals or clean up afterward. Some of the guys learned enough about cooking to get jobs in restaurants once they got out.

Bowmanville was tough, but definitely not a hellhole. If it became anything like a hellhole, it was of your own making. The guards were strict, but if you kept your nose clean you were treated pretty well. What they were trying to do at Bowmanville was to give us a disciplined, regimented environment—

something none of us had ever had. It was definitely a rehabilitation and training center. If you wanted to turn it into a place of punishment, that was your choice.

At night there were informal sports, games, and competition at the main gym, or you could stay in your barracks' lounge and listen to the radio or play pool. Saturday was movie night and considered the highlight of the week. We seldom saw any first-run pictures. It was mostly Class B westerns, comedies, and cops-and-robbers pictures that always showed the bad guys getting caught.

In my first couple of weeks at Bowmanville, I learned a lot about the place—how all the fences and buildings were laid out. Adjoining the main reception detention house and the barracks houses were the hospital, the shops, and the class-room buildings. At the far end of the compound were a laundry, barber shop, and clothing repair center. Next door was the leather department, where I would eventually spend a great deal of my time learning to make shoes, moccasins, and all kinds of leather goods.

The whole compound was surrounded by a twelve-foot wire fence with two strings of barbed wire on top. In front of the main building was a shallow ravine with a creek running through it that we dammed up in the summer for swimming. Across a bridge was the farm area where they kept the cattle and the horses. There were also huge fields where they grew potatoes, tomatoes, and other crops. The entire property was surrounded by still more fence. The Bowmanville facility covered several hundred acres in all.

I also became well acquainted with the Digger because I had such a short fuse. It was easy to get me going—a shove while lining up to march to the dining hall would usually set me off. I arrived at Bowmanville early in October, and during my first few weeks I was sent to the Digger at least four times. I even celebrated my thirteenth birthday—on October 22—in the Digger.

Because I had seen so many movies, I knew all about convicts "breaking out of the pen," and I decided I would give it a try. I made my first attempt on the snowy night of November 11 after learning the complete layout of my barracks' building and making careful plans. After shower time that evening, I hung behind in the locker room area, and when everyone was gone, I grabbed my clothes, including my jacket, and ducked into the broom closet near the showers.

In the floor of the broom closet was a metal grate, which opened into a large sewer drain, easily big enough for me to wiggle through. I crawled through the drain, under the twelve-foot fence, into a field, and headed for the highway. A couple of guys had told me that was how to get away—make it to the highway and hitch a ride.

The guards soon missed me at bed check and figured out what I had done. They tracked me in the snow and caught me before I reached Highway 1 just outside of Bowmanville. They didn't rough me up or anything but just brought me back, warning me that if I tried it again I'd be in real trouble. And, of course, I was back in the Digger for at least two days.

I didn't try escaping again until the end of November, and this time I took a much simpler route. During free time on Sunday some of the guys were hanging out in a "smoke circle," puffing on their homemade cigarettes. Others were in boxing matches, which attracted a lot of attention. I wandered down toward the horticulture building and then along a road that went toward some of the crop fields.

I couldn't believe my luck! The gate wasn't even locked, and nobody was guarding it! I walked right on through and down the road until I got to some bushes. I cut off the road, found the railroad tracks, and started walking along the tracks, heading away from Bowmanville. One of the guys had told me that if I followed the tracks long enough I would come to a highway. And I almost made it, but as I came around a bend, there was a car sitting in an opening next to the tracks!

I tried to run, but they caught me. One of the guards, who wore leather gloves, decided to give me a few good punches in the back with his fists. He had been a boxer and was sort of a sadist anyway. He later got fired for being too rough, but he didn't get caught that night. He worked me over pretty good, but he knew where to punch so no one could tell.

They hauled me back and threw me into the Digger again, this time for five days. As I sat in that tiny cubicle, with only a glimmer of light coming under the door, I vowed I'd get out of Bowmanville somehow. Being caged like some animal in the Detroit Zoo was not my idea of being alive, and if I had to die, so would some of the guards!

Two escape attempts and two failures put two strikes on me, in more ways than one. Everytime I tried escaping, the staff would retaliate by taking away the privileges of my entire barracks. This did not make me very popular with the rest of the group, which included some very mean dudes. There were about eight of them in one particular clique who sort of ran the place. They decided that they would "teach me a lesson" because they were sick and tired of losing their smoking privileges due to my escape attempts. I wasn't the only one trying to escape, but in their minds I would make a good scapegoat, and they waited for their chance.

One night as I was coming out of the shower, somebody shoved me from behind and I slammed into the shower wall. I never really knew who or what hit me, but I woke up in the hospital with a broken left arm, a broken nose, and smashed lips. Somehow I still had all my teeth.

I had been warned, and later I was told just who had jumped me because they "ran North House." One of the tough guys was a huge guy with a bull neck who went by the name of Junky Jinx. Another big guy in their gang had a huge nose and looked like a Greek. Because we had a Greek restaurant in Sarnia named Zorba, I decided I'd call him Zorba—but not to his face!

The leader of the tough-guy pack was a guy named Larry with long, blond hair. He was probably the most dangerous of all. A sadist, he was definitely a little unbalanced. He used to find a piece of electrical wire, strip off the insulation, and fray the tip so it bristled with hundreds of razor sharp points. Then he'd wrap the frayed wire around his wrists and hide it under the cuff of his jacket. When he got in a fight, he would slip the wire up from beneath his cuff and use it to slash people to ribbons.

Larry eventually got caught and was thrown in the Digger for several days. In fact, he was caught by Mr. Woods, the guard I had coldcocked back in Cobourg. Mr. Woods had been transferred to Bowmanville and had been put in charge of the reception house. He was still able to work, even though I had partially crippled him with those doorknobs. He was really a gentle guy—very trusting—in his later forties or early fifties, which to me seemed ancient. He had been in the war in the Royal Air Force. When he learned I was in Bowmanville, he never threatened me or even said anything mean or abusive. I guess somehow he had forgiven me for what I had done to him.

While Larry and the rest of his gang had sent me a message, they didn't realize I was planning to send back one of my own. Because I couldn't take on all eight of them at once, I bided my

time, scheming how I could pick them off one by one. My first
chance came the following spring when we formed an informal
softball league. In order to keep things even, they would mix
guys up so a team would have players from North House,
Center House, South House, and so on.

One day Jinx was catching for another team—*without a
mask.* I stepped up to the plate and he kept taunting me, "You'll
never hit it, Powers. You bat like a girl anyway. . . ."

I just smiled and gripped the old baseball bat all the harder.
The pitch came in, and I whacked the ball out into center field.
But instead of dropping the bat the way hitters normally do, I
threw it behind me, swinging it with all my might and letting it
fly directly into Jinx's face. It smashed his nose, loosened his
teeth, and knocked him cold. I started running toward first
base, but then I stopped, looked back, and saw Jinx on the
ground. I acted shocked because of the "accident" and said I
felt bad for what I had done "by mistake."

The guards who were umpiring rushed over. One of them
asked me why I had swung the bat that way.

"I don't . . . I don't know," I stammered. "I was excited because I got a hit and I just let go of it, I guess." Jinx knew better
and so did the guys in his gang, but because no one could
prove anything, I didn't get punished. I kept my eyes open for
possible retaliation by Larry, Zorba, or one of Jinx's other
buddies, but none came. After they had beaten me up in the
shower room, someone had squealed, and they all had lost
privileges for a long time. I guessed they just weren't interested
in going through all that again.

My second victim that summer was Zorba, and this time the
swimming pool was the scene of my crime. I had just finished
taking a shower, which was mandatory before going into the
pool, and as I came over to the shallow edge, there was Zorba,
doing some kind of underwater maneuver in only three feet of
water. Without hesitating I jumped in, feet first, landing on his
back and shoving his chest and face into the rough bottom of
the pool. He came up bruised and bloody, choking and sputter-
ing, and had to get treated at the infirmary.

Because there were strict rules against jumping carelessly
into the pool, I got punished for that one. I was grounded with
extra kitchen duty, and I also spent a day in the Digger, but it
was worth it. The word was getting around, and I was gaining

some respect among the guys. They would whisper, "You don't want to mess with Powers—he's one crazy hard rock!"

That fall I was taking my turn on kitchen duty and was assigned to wash the trays and silverware. Larry, the psycho, was in charge of scalding all the dishes, and when he looked up, there I was, grinning at him. For awhile a lot of words went back and forth about what we were going to do to each other, but I just kept smiling and taunting him.

Our dialogue went on for about an hour, and then Larry lost his cool, picked up a big butcher knife, and came after me. I grabbed a giant soup ladle and fended him off. Some of the kitchen staff workers heard the commotion and came running, but before they got there Larry slipped on some water and dropped the knife. I grabbed it and swiped at his arm, cutting him slightly.

Larry screamed, and as the guards tried to pull me off, he rolled over and tried to kick me. I slashed at his boot with the knife, but somehow it missed his foot and caught him in the stomach, opening him up pretty good. Larry didn't die, but he was seriously hurt, and it took a lot of stitches to close the wound.

Word spread like wildfire about my battle with Larry, and I was immediately dubbed, "Crazy Powers." My "vicious knife attack" on Larry convinced the Bowmanville staff that I was just too dangerous to be around kids my age. By the next day I was sent to Guelph—a reform school for older guys, sixteen to twenty, located about sixty miles west of Toronto, not far from Sarnia.

It was just as well. I knew if I had stayed at Bowmanville somebody would have wound up dead, and it might have been me!

SIX

"SEND HIM TO HELL, FOR ALL I CARE!"

"I don't care what you say . . . I don't give a . . . You can all go to
. . . I'll kill myself before I'll stay in here!"

When I got to Guelph, outbursts like that got me labeled
suicidal, and I was put under what they called "watchful care."
In other words, I was dangerous to myself as well as others and
had to be observed constantly. For awhile I was held in a room
that had a door with a glass window and allowed no belt, shoes,
or tie. Somebody was always watching me through that window,
and I just sat there making faces and laughing at all those stupid
jerks.

Guelph was more like a prison, with a high brick wall at least
two stories high with barbed wire on top. It was full of really bad
guys, but I never had to be around them. Inside the main facility
was the Ontario Trade School, sort of a prison within a greater
prison, and that's where I spent the next four or five months,
much of it in solitary confinement.

And that's when I broke. The guards at Guelph found a way to
get to me, not with beatings or tongue lashings, but with silence.
They just wouldn't talk to me, and I was left completely alone
for hours and days at a time. I was terrified, and while I didn't
cry, I still broke down. First I screamed and pounded and
shouted, and then I just sort of withdrew and said nothing. From
the first day, however, the guards never spoke, not even when
serving me my meals. After several weeks of this, I started
begging them: "Please talk . . . say something . . . chew me out
. . . cuss me out . . . *anything!*"

Finally one of the guards walked over and said, "So, Powers, you're ready to talk?"

"Yeah . . . I guess so."

"How do you feel?"

"Like crap," I snapped.

"And so you want me to talk to you?" he asked again. I wondered if he was taunting me or something.

"Yeah, I *said* I wanted to talk. What more do you want from me?"

The guard smiled and said, "OK, Powers . . . we'll talk to you. In fact, I've got a lot of things I want to talk about. . . ."

After that, this same guard would talk to me often. I don't remember his name, but I remember our conversations. He would come by my table, sit down, and we would talk. He had a quiet way about him, but there was still something underneath that said, *Don't monkey with me, or you'll pay.*

I had always been able to size up the guards and sense what they were made of. You could tell by the way they looked at you whether they were mean or not. The ones who were mean would always find a way to get at you if you crossed them. Sometimes it was under the table by grinding your toes under the heel of their shoe. Sometimes they'd get you in the knees, or the sides, or they'd just shove you against the door frame as you walked through it. There were all kinds of ways to jar you or bump you and bruise you, to let you know who was boss.

I could tell that this guy had all the tricks and then some. But for some reason, he also wanted to get through to me. His basic message was, "Look, Powers, you're Mr. Tough Guy, but you've seen a lot of the movies, and just remember that in the end, the tough guy always gets killed."

We talked about how I had killed the old lady, and was I sorry? I didn't need to hurt Mr. Woods, so why had I smashed him on the head and crippled him for the rest of his life? And what about the three guys who I tried to kill because they had beaten me up? I let the guard know I really didn't want to kill them—I just wanted to get even.

Obviously he'd gotten my file from the office and had read it thoroughly. He knew all about me. And then he told me, "Powers, you've got an opportunity when you get out of here. But I don't think you're going to make it. You'll be dead in no time because you're stupid."

That irritated me because I knew I wasn't stupid and I told him so.

"Yes—you *are* stupid. You know what your problem is? You can't control *you,* and you're not going to make it. Remember what I said about the tough guys and the gangsters? In the end they always get killed. I've seen it too many times."

"Not me," I sneered.

The guard just laughed, a short, brittle laugh and then looked hard and deep into my eyes: "I've heard that hundreds of times too. I'm telling you, Powers, we're shipping you back to Bowmanville, but I don't think you have much going for you. And the next time you step over the line, you're dead meat because they're going to smack you right into Whitby."

I didn't admit it to the guard, but *that* got my attention. Whitby was an institution for the criminally insane with padded cells and all the rest. It was not too far from Bowmanville, and when I had been in jail at Sarnia, I had worried about being sent to Whitby because everybody thought a kid of twelve who could shoot an old lady had to be crazy.

In less than a week I was back at Bowmanville, but that guard's words still rang in my ears. If I were ever sent to Whitby, they'd put me in one of those padded cells, and I'd never be able to talk to anyone again. I knew from my experience at Guelph that I had to have somebody to argue with, to holler at, to talk to. It was part of my makeup, and I couldn't do without it.

I came back to Bowmanville in July of 1951, and by then I'd made my decision. I would play the game. I would get out of there, but I would do it "the right way" by working up from blue tie to green, then to red, and, finally, probation. I would go to school and try to learn to read and catch up on all the stuff I had missed because of skipping so much school back in Sarnia.

As for Larry and his gang, they posed no big threat any more. Junky Jinx had worked himself up to a red tie and gotten out while I was at Guelph. I always figured he went on to a career as a wrestler, or maybe an enforcer for a loan shark in Toronto. Larry and Zorba were still there but had been transferred to maximum security in Center House. I was put back in North House, and I had little to do with them.

Some new prisoners had come in while I was gone—some really tough black guys from the Windsor area across the border from Detroit. And there was one Indian from Stag Island, where we had often stashed our loot before we sold it to the factory workers along the St. Clair River. I had known his brother, and I could tell he was one rough character.

One of those big black kids from Windsor was named Wilson. He was in for car theft and breaking and entering. As we sat around shooting the breeze, he would often say, "It's all the way you say 'Yes, Massah.' You make fun of the guard and he know it and you're in trouble. But I'm not dumb. You wanna stay in here and get your head beaten in, you can be a smart mouth, but if you answer nice and roll over when they want you to, you'll get out." I listened to Wilson because I knew from experience he was right. He had been around, in and out of Bowmanville and other places two or three times.

So I kept my nose clean and stayed out of trouble. I knew I had to make it, and I was determined to do so. I got back into trying to do schoolwork and wound up in a combination of grades four and five. Frankly, though, I never made much progress with reading or anything else that had to do with books. But manual arts was a different story. I began working in the laundry and earned a Certificate of Merit that said I knew how to handle three different machines.

I also started doing leather hobby craft—making belts, neckties, and things like that. The leather teacher who ran the hobby sessions at night was Mr. Vanderhoff, a pencil-thin Dutchman with narrow shoulders who had emigrated to Canada from Holland. Mr. Vanderhoff was strict, but he was also kindly and encouraging. He saw that I had creative abilities and suggested that I get into a formal leather-making class where I would learn to make slippers and moccasins and repair shoes.

In leather class I found my niche! I liked stripping down a pair of shoes that needed resoling, turning the leather on the lathe, and putting on midsoles and heels. I especially loved the smell—that pungent odor became comfortable and familiar to me. Mr. Vanderhoff liked my work and would encourage me with comments like, "That's good, LaVern, that's creative . . . by the way, I've got another book you might be interested in . . . why don't you try doing this?"

Later Mr. Vanderhoff would be the one to recommend to my probation officer that maybe a shoe factory would be the best place for me to try to get a job once I got out of Bowmanville. Throughout that fall and winter, life went better for me because I was learning and finally somebody was paying attention to me, telling me that I could do good things, creative things—that I wasn't stupid.

In a few months, I had worked my way up to green tie and was eligible for a few more privileges. One of those privileges was projecting films for the entire school. I had learned something about movie projectors back in Sarnia when I was ten and eleven years old. A guy I went to school with had an uncle who was a projectionist at the Capitol Theatre. One Saturday after the movie we went upstairs in the back and hung around while he showed us how the projectors worked. Because I was handy with things like that, I caught on quickly and came back frequently to learn a little more each time.

Eventually the guy would leave me in charge while he slipped across the alley to the Colonial Hotel to get a drink. I learned to run the big 35-mm machines that projected the major movies, as well as the 16-mm that they used for shorts and advertisements. I learned how to thread the projector, how to rewind the film, how to keep it clean, and even how to patch tears and breaks. But of course I had never stuck with it. Being in the gang, stealing, and getting in fights seemed to be a lot more fun.

On the Saturday night after I had earned my green tie, I was watching movies with the rest of the guys, but the film kept breaking. The staff person in charge of showing films was one of the classroom teachers and really wasn't that crazy about the job. He knew just enough to put the film in the projector, but that was about all.

While he was fiddling with the broken film, I called up to the projection booth and said, "I can help you—I can fix that." The teacher looked out the little window, down at me, and said, "If you think you can do a better job, Powers, put up or shut up!"

All the guys in the room laughed and made fun of me. How could anybody with a girl's name fix anything? But I just gave everyone a disgusted look and went up the short stairway to the projection booth. As I came through the door, the teacher wasn't too thrilled to see me! I could see that he was trying to splice the film but wasn't doing it correctly.

He had been using some kind of scraper, but I knew sandpaper worked better, and I asked him for some. When he got me the sandpaper, I rubbed the edges of the break to make a better fit and to get better adhesion for a proper splice. And then, when we glued the film, I told him we had to *wait* for about three minutes. That really made the big difference because the glue had a chance to dry properly. Normally—because all the guys were hollering, hooting, and getting impatient—the teacher would just glue it, slap it back on the machine, and start up the movie again. But I insisted that we wait three minutes no matter how impatient they got because it would pay off—and it did!

The film ran fine for the rest of the evening. And while the teacher was irritated because a smart young punk like Powers could do something he couldn't do, I think he was secretly grateful because I really made life simpler for him. For the next several weeks I helped him every Saturday night. I found out he liked to drink, and he also "liked boys," but I let him know I was *not* available, and knowing my reputation, he never tried anything again after he made that first pass.

Every Saturday I'd come early and we would run the films through the projector slowly—by hand. I would hold the film between my fingers with a piece of Kleenex to clean it and to feel for any broken sprocket holes or other problems. When I discovered one, we'd stop and I would repair the broken holes with Scotch tape, or, if necessary, we would make a new splice where the film was about to break.

I also asked him to get some rubbing alcohol so we could clean the film as well as the gates of the projector where dirt would always accumulate. He liked the alcohol part. I saw him take a nip of the stuff every now and then, but even though I'd practically been an alcoholic myself on the outside, I never did try any rubbing alcohol.

Eventually I became the unofficial projectionist for Bowmanville Training School for Boys. Anytime a film was to be shown, I was called on to do it, not only on Saturday nights but during the weekdays too, when educational films were used in classes. I wasn't much for the regular classroom subjects, mostly because I never learned to read very well. But whenever someone showed me how to do something with my hands, I usually caught on the first time and could handle it from there.

By March 1952 I'd worked my way up to a red tie, and the time came for a probation hearing. By then I was really going great in the leather department. I was sixteen, ready to get out on my own and find a job in a shoe factory somewhere—if I could.

My probation hearing was held in the office of J. J. Brown, the director of Bowmanville. Mr. Moses, the teacher of my regular schoolwork classes, was there, and so was Mr. Vanderhoff, the leather teacher. Also there was a guard called "Smitty" who had done a lot of overseeing in my barracks. Another man present would be my probation officer if and when I got out. His name was Mr. Cuthbertson.

One other man entered the room—my father, whom I had not seen since I had been sent to Bowmanville almost three years before. During my entire time in reform school, no one from my family ever paid me a visit.

It was one of the few times I had ever seen my father sober. Those flat grey eyes seemed to look right through me, and then he sat down with his back to me, never even bothering to say hello. Mr. Brown read from my record, noting all my accomplishments and the good progress I had made. Finally, he turned to my father and said, "Mr. Powers, we don't believe it would be in LaVern's best interests to be returned to his home environment. But we do have some other alternatives as to where he can be sent. . . ."

My father stared silently at Mr. Brown for several seconds. Then he muttered, "I don't care . . . *send him to hell, for all I care. . . .*"

My father's words seared my brain like a hot iron. I was sitting in a big wooden armchair. I would have come straight to my feet and lunged at my father, but Smitty was sitting on my left and Mr. Cuthbertson was on my right. They both clamped down on my hands, pinning them to the arms of the chair.

Smitty's dark eyes bored into mine, and his look said, *Cool it, Powers. Don't screw up now!* Somehow I understood. I bit off the scream of rage that was in my throat, but my thoughts shouted, *I'll kill you, you drunken jerk!*

My father's rejection totally stunned me. I thought he would take me home or do something to get me out of there. At least he could have said, "I'd like to help you, but I just can't—there's no way they'll let me take you home, and I'm sorry." But he didn't even care enough to turn around, look me in the eye, and say hello. He just sat there, staring straight ahead, saying nothing.

Mr. Brown sighed, shuffled some papers, then turned to Mr. Cuthbertson and said, "LaVern will be placed in your charge, and it will be up to you to find him suitable placement—a better environment."

As Mr. Cuthbertson led me from the room, I stared at my father's back, vowing revenge: *I'll kill you! Someday, somehow, I'll kill you! Someday, somehow, I'll get out of here! And when I do, you're dead!*

SEVEN

"WE CARE ABOUT YOUR FUTURE, NOT YOUR PAST!"

"Send him to hell . . . *Send him to hell . . . !*" My father's words roared in my ears as I left the probation hearing. Mr. Cuthbertson let me go into the bathroom, where I swore, pounded, and screamed aloud what I would try to do to my father someday.

But I never cried. Crying was a luxury that I had chosen to do without because "real men don't cry, babies cry."

Smitty and Mr. Cuthbertson waited outside the bathroom until I was through. When I came out, Smitty said, "Have you got it out of your system?" I just glared at him, and Cuthbertson invited me to get some coffee over in the kitchen. We sat down and he said, "LaVern, I've got to plan your future."

"What future? I've played the game, kept my nose clean, rolled over and barked just the way you all wanted me to, and what's it gotten me?"

"No, no," Cuthbertson said. "You have to think differently. You've been going great. Forget about your father for now. You don't need that. You've got potential—you've got it LaVern; you've got potential."

I looked long and hard at Cuthbertson, and the frustration of years of bad luck, abuse, and violence spilled out.

"Yeah, just *look* at my potential. My mother dies, and my stepmother does her hustling in the upstairs bedroom. My father drinks and smashes me to pieces. My brother stabs me because he catches me stealing from his wallet. My sister kicks me out of the second story window because she catches me robbing her purse. I've been shot by zip guns, busted up with baseball bats—once my stepmother even knifed me in my hand when I reached for a piece of chicken. Yeah, I'm just *loaded* with potential . . . !"

Cuthbertson sat there listening impassively. When my outburst was over, he finished his coffee, stood up, and smiled. "LaVern, you've had a rough life—maybe one of the roughest I've ever heard about, but we're not going to let that stop us. I still think you've got potential, and we're going to get you out of here."

Mr. Cuthbertson was as good as his word. In less than a week, he told me to pack my bag. "We've got some interviews, LaVern," he said cheerfully, "and not too far away."

As we headed through the reformatory gate, I asked, "Where are we going?"

"To a place called Batawa, about sixty-five miles east of here," he answered. "It's the home of Bata Shoes—they're world-famous, and one of their best factories is at Batawa."

As we drove along, Cuthbertson explained a little more about Bata Shoes and Batawa, a little village of almost three hundred people, completely owned by the company. They had built small houses for the families who worked at the factory. It was a "company town" in every sense of the word, but people were happy because Bata treated its employees fairly and paid adequate wages.

We got to the factory just after lunch and went in to talk to Mr. English, the personnel manager. Cuthbertson had also told me that if I didn't get hired, we'd go back to Bowmanville and then go out and try again in other places that he had lined up. As we sat down in Mr. English's office, I kept telling myself, *They won't hire me . . . they don't want me—nobody wants me, not even my own father.*

Mr. English looked over my file, noting that I showed promise as a worker with leather, and then he said, "Well, LaVern, we can put you to work here, but there's one problem. I have no place for you to stay. There's the boarding house that the company oversees, but it's full and I don't know anybody who would take you on a room-and-board basis. We can hire you . . . you can have a job and start tomorrow, and I'm sure you'd work your way in with these qualifications, but I just don't know any place where you can stay right now."

My heart sank, and anger welled up in my chest at the same time. It was just as I thought. *There will never be any place for me . . . who would want someone like LaVern Powers anyway?*

At that moment the phone rang. Mr. English picked it up and said, "I told you, no calls unless it's an emergency." He listened for a moment and then said, "Well, OK, in that case I'll take it. . . . Hello, Mrs. Adams? How are you?"

He listened for well over a minute and finally murmured, "Hmmm . . . isn't that interesting," as he gave Mr. Cuthbertson a knowing look. "Uh-huh . . . well, I just might have somebody for you . . . I'm glad you called because I was just in a situation . . . sure, Mrs. Adams, right . . . I'll be sending him right over."

He hung up and turned to us and explained, "The lady who just called is from Frankford, and her two sons work here. Joe Adams is head of the cutting room, and Lloyd is also one of the cutters . . . their father used to work here with us as a security guard. She just called to ask if there was anybody they could take into their home on a room-and-board basis. Their son, Lloyd, would be glad to pick you up every day, take you to work, and then bring you home, because he works the same shift you would."

"Well!" said Cuthbertson. "That's what I call timing! Let's go, LaVern."

We got directions to Mrs. Adams's house and drove over to Frankford, a small town of maybe a thousand people, about four miles north of Batawa. I liked the place immediately. Frankford lay along the Trent Canal and had lots of big maple trees that were just starting to bud. We drove up to the house, right across from the United Church. It was a big, white two-story place, with a pillared veranda, which looked a lot more inviting than the front gate of Bowmanville.

We knocked and a voice called from inside, "Come on in!" We walked right into a large kitchen, and I saw Mrs. Adams for the first time. She was sitting in front of her kitchen stove in a rocking chair—with her feet in the oven! She said, "Come on in, Son, come on in . . . it's OK."

Mrs. Adams was a tiny woman, not even five feet tall, and she couldn't have weighed more than eighty pounds soaking wet. She wore a long black dress and black stockings, and her little white lace collar came up around her face. Her grey hair was in a bun, and she had wrinkles on wrinkles. She was in her late sixties but looked a lot older than that to me. Yet I noticed that her eyes twinkled as she greeted us.

I started chuckling to myself inside. This old bird was going to tell *me* what to do? One good sneeze and she'd crack into a million pieces. She looked like a dried-out version of Whistler's Mother, but instead of sitting by the fireplace, she had her feet in the oven! It was really hilarious, and I almost snickered out loud.

Mrs. Adams pulled her feet out of the oven, slipped on some shoes, and said, "Sit down, I'll get you some tea." We sat at the kitchen table as she used a cane to rustle around finding tea and cookies. Then she served us, sat down, and said, "And how are you, Sonny? You're the boy that we're going to have. Oh, we're so glad! We want to thank the Lord for you."

It was all I could do to keep from laughing in her face. Above the refrigerator was a picture of Jesus standing at some door and knocking. Over by the radio was another picture of Christ, and near it was a little wall plaque with a prayer:

> *Cheer up!*
> *The Son hasn't gone out of business.*

On still another wall was another plaque:

> *Of all your troubles, great or small,*
> *The greatest of those never happened at all!*

I was doing my best not to laugh out loud, but she must have seen the smirk on my face. I thought to myself, *You old fossil . . . I could break your cane and then what would you do?*

"Clarence, Clarence, dear . . . ," she called out. "I want you to meet my husband," she told us. I found out later her name was Clara. Clara and Clarence—it fit.

But in the next few seconds there were some creaking noises, and the house almost seemed to shake a bit. Cuthbertson and I turned to look at the kitchen doorway, which was suddenly completely filled by Clarence. He was at least six-foot-two and must have weighed nearly three hundred pounds, much of which was *not* fat! He had been a security police officer for the Bata Shoe Company, and, even in his early seventies, he still stood ramrod straight. His huge hands looked awfully strong, and my snickers turned to shivers. All I could think of was *King Kong!* Breaking Mrs. Adams' cane suddenly seemed like a very bad idea.

Cuthbertson reached under the table and gave me a knowing poke as Clarence pulled a stout looking chair up to the table and sat down. "Well," his deep voice rumbled, "and how are you doing, Sonny?"

"OK," I mumbled as Cuthbertson reached in his briefcase and pulled out my file.

He said to the Adams, "I think I should tell you some things about LaVern so you know his background. I brought him here from Bowmanville Reform School. . . ." And then he went on with his pitch, letting them know what supervising me would be like. I would pay room and board, and he would come by to see me every three months. I'd also have to report to the local police at least once a month.

Clarence finally interrupted Cuthbertson and said, "Doesn't look like the type."

Cuthbertson paused, looking surprised, "Doesn't look like what type?"

"Well, to be in reform school," Clarence answered. "Doesn't look like the type. All we know is, we prayed, and this is the son that God has given us. All our kids are grown . . . this is our new son."

"I'm nobody's son," I snapped. "I'm nobody's son. . . ."

"You've got to have a daddy to be alive," Mrs. Adams murmured.

"Like hell," I snapped.

Mrs. Adams ignored that remark and turned to Mr. Cuthbertson and said, "We've raised our family. They're gone and have children of their own. We were praying in our devotions this morning and thought we still had some love to give someone."

Then she turned, reached across the table, patted my hand, and said something that I will never forget: "Sonny, we don't care about your past, *we only care about what God's going to do for your future.*"

That threw me for a second, but then I looked over at Cuthbertson and back to them and said, "I'm not religious, and I'm not a Catholic."

"Neither are we," she said cheerfully. "We believe in Jesus. We hope you will."

I turned to Cuthbertson and asked him almost irritably, "Do I *have* to stay here?"

"No," he said thoughtfully, "and they don't have to take you, either."

Mrs. Adams got up from the table saying, "We would really like to have you if you'll stay. You'll have a real nice room all to yourself. Let me take you upstairs and show you."

As we climbed the stairs, I noticed that Mrs. Adams was pretty spry for someone who used a cane. It turned out she needed it only occasionally when her arthritis acted up. First she showed me the bathroom, which actually had a door you could lock! At Bowmanville the bathrooms had been doorless, as were all the toilets. Then she took me across the hall to what seemed to be a huge room with a big bed and a dresser. There was a window, and I could see a big hill beyond the backyard. Green grass and trees were everywhere. Suddenly I knew I didn't want to go back to reform school!

"Now, just so we understand ourselves, Son, what's your name?"

"LaVern," I said sullenly.

Mrs. Adams looked at me hard and said, "There's a lot of hate there, LaVern. You can't live that way. Please stay here . . . we need you." Then she walked away a few feet and started to cry.

I wanted to cry, too, but I wasn't going to be any sucker. She had no right to pull this on me. What was she trying to do, anyway? She came back over to me and said, "You know, I've just been thinking. You're a much younger man than I thought . . . maybe this room is too old-fashioned for you. Is there anything you don't like?"

I thought, *Now's my chance to give this old bird a hard time.* I reeled off a list of things I didn't like—the lacy bedspread, the dresser with the doilie on top . . . there was no radio, and I didn't like the religious pictures or the little God Bless Our Home sign on one wall.

She listened, but instead of getting angry, she just said, "All right, we can change all that."

We went back downstairs, and Mr. Cuthbertson could see that I was probably going to stay. Mrs. Adams said, "You know, I suppose a young person like you probably watches television . . . do you like hockey?"

"I'm not into sports," I said. "I like a good mystery, or comedy . . . something you can laugh at."

"I think our son Lloyd has an extra television set, and we just might bring it over here."

It turned out the Adams never watched TV. They just listened to the radio and she often played the piano. I also learned later that she was Honorary President of the Young People's Society of the Church of the Nazarene in Trenton, another small town a few miles to the south. She played the piano for some of their meetings, and young people attended from the Nazarene church as well as the Free Methodist church in Frankford. She'd have parties for them, even counsel them, and they loved her.

Her relationship to the young people in the area helped explain why she had accepted me and my surly ways from the start. Most little old ladies would have been so repulsed by the way I acted that I would have been out of there in five minutes. But not Mrs. Adams. I was there, and she wasn't going to give ground, no matter how nasty I was. God had sent me, and, as far as she was concerned, I was their new son. But I didn't like that name, "Son."

"Don't you call me 'Son,' " I told them. I just didn't feel like anybody's son.

I agreed to give the Adamses' place a try. Cuthbertson put it on a three-month basis, and then he'd be back to see what had happened. And I said OK. I sort of liked the old lady and her husband, but they bothered me, too, with all their religious knickknacks and talking about God so much. But what really clinched it was, *I didn't want to go back to Bowmanville.* The view from that bedroom window upstairs was much better than the one from North House.

I started to work at the Bata Shoe Factory the next day—that is, I started doing the job they gave me. I came in with all my training and skill in leather and fully expected to be put right into making shoes. Instead, they put me on the third floor in the rubber department—sticking little rubber ankle patches on running shoes!

I thought it was the most boring job in the whole world. My instructions were to place the upper part of the running shoe in the slot of the machine, slip in a little rubber patch about the size of a checker, and then bring down the arm that would apply heat that "vulcanized" the patch onto the ankle area of the shoe, engraving the words *Bata Shoes* into the patch at the same time.

So instead of making shoes, I started out by decorating them—but at least I was out of prison, making my own money, eating three good meals a day, and even getting over to local bars now and then for a drink. I could also buy my own cigarettes—real ones, not those crummy roll-your-owns.

I was also able to get some new clothes instead of having to wear that same red tie every day. When I got out, the reformatory had given me fifty dollars spending money. That was a start, but the real thrill was my first paycheck—twenty-five dollars, after taxes, and for only a week's work! I only had to pay ten dollars a week room and board to the Adamses, so with fifteen dollars to spare, I thought I was rich!

As for living with Clarence and Clara Adams, that had its pros and cons. I had my own room and the view of the hill from the window. When I was at the house, I stayed in my room most of the time, but she still would drive me crazy by playing the piano and singing hymns that I could hear all the way up the stairs: "What a Friend We Have in Jesus," "Shall We Gather at the River?" "Mansion over the Hilltop," and one that used to really bug me—"I'd Rather Have Jesus Than Silver or Gold."

They also prayed before meals, so I had to hear prayers twice a day at breakfast and dinner. At least I could eat lunch in peace down at the factory! After a couple of weeks at the Adamses', I had heard more religious songs and prayers than I'd ever heard in my entire life. All I'd ever gotten at home was Betty's ranting and raving against the church.

In reform school, one of my few "religious experiences" had happened one Christmas when the Gideons came. We didn't know they were the Gideons. It was Christmas Day, and word had gotten around that a guy was going to give away cigarettes. A lot of us would do anything for a factory-made cigarette—even go to some kind of religious Christmas program. So we marched from our barracks to the rec hall and sat in our respective groups, waiting to see what would happen. I was right in the front row, and up on the platform was a piano and a table filled with little white packages with blue ribbons.

The guy from the Gideons stepped up on the platform and said, "Hello, boys, welcome to our Christmas program!"

We all booed in unison, while the guards sat out in the back hallway having a smoke.

Unruffled, the man went over to the table, picked up one of

the little white packages and said, "Who would like to be first to get one of these?"

This wasn't going to be so bad after all. He hadn't even prayed, or talked about anything religious. Apparently, all he wanted to do was to give us a gift.

I was right by the steps to the stage—I didn't plan it that way, but I happened to be there. And when he said, "Who'd like to be first?"—*bang!*—I was up there. I grabbed the package out of his hand, but he said, "Wait a minute, we want to thank you for coming to our program." I looked at him and shrugged as if to say, "Big deal." He made everyone else sit down—there were dozens of other guys ready to rush the stage—and he asked me my name.

"LaVern," I told him, and of course all the guys in the audience started hooting and making fun. The guy from the Gideons almost laughed, too, but then he composed himself and said, "Would you like to open your package?"

I thought, *Why not? I'll show these guys that I got the first package of smokes.* So I opened the package, but instead of cigarettes it contained a little red book!

"What in the . . . is this?" I demanded.

"Don't you know what it is?" the man asked.

"If I knew what it was, I wouldn't have to ask you . . . it's a bloody little book with writing so small I can't even read it."

Then the guy said, "It's the New Testament."

By this time almost everybody in the room was just roaring. Some of them knew what a New Testament was, but I had no idea. The only time I had ever seen a Bible was when we robbed the poor box in the Catholic church in Sarnia. And once in the Baptist church, we broke into the office and stole money out of the desk. There was always a great big Bible sitting at the front of the church, but I had never even looked inside of one.

At this point I started giving the guy a few chosen words, but all he said was, "Don't you understand that it talks about how God loves you?"

"Nobody loves me," I almost shouted.

"God loves you—that's what Christmas is all about."

"No, all Christmas is, is candy and Santa Claus!"

"Don't you like Christmas?"

"No . . ." I paused and then said almost in a whisper, "That's when my mama died."

I could hear some of the guys in the front row snickering, and then I really got mad. I didn't want his New Testament, so I ripped it up and threw it in his face. All the guys started to cheer and shout, and the guards moved in. They took all of us back to our barracks, so nobody got a New Testament that day.

Before I started living with the Adamses, I hadn't heard two sentences out of the Bible. Now I was hearing it every morning during something they called "devotions," just after breakfast. Besides reading out of a big, black Bible, they also had a "Promise Box," which contained little cards with Bible verses printed on them. They'd each take one and read it, and they'd ask me to take one and read it too, but I seldom did. Usually I'd sit there with a bored look on my face, but it never seemed to bother them. They were always happy and cheerful and seemed to really know this God they kept praying to.

But I didn't want to know him . . . he'd never done anything for me . . . he hadn't kept my real mom from dying . . . and he'd never helped me out of any scrapes. As far as I was concerned, I didn't need God, and he had no use for me either.

EIGHT
My Magic Turns to Witchcraft

During my first few months at Frankford, I was frugal with my money and soon had saved up enough to buy a car. One day Mr. Adams took me down to a used car lot in Frankford, just off Highway 401. He knew the owner and helped me pick out a '35 Dodge coupe for fifty-two dollars. Because I was over sixteen, the legal age to drive in Ontario, I had no trouble getting a license.

After that I was really on my own, able to drive over to Belleville or Trenton anytime I wanted to get a drink. I was well under twenty-one, the legal age for drinking, but I looked older, and the bars I went to never asked any questions.

I had a lot of fun in those bars. They were comfortable, and the people there liked to watch me do card or coin tricks. Back at Bowmanville I had managed to keep practicing the tricks I learned from that book I was given in the Sarnia jail. Eventually somebody stole the book from me at Bowmanville, but by then I knew the tricks. I would practice them now and then—usually when I could be by myself. Since I had the rep for being weird anyhow, most people gave me a wide berth, and I'd get off in a corner somewhere and do my thing with cards or coins. I think a lot of guys just thought, *There's Powers again . . . he thinks he's a magician . . . he's got to be crazy!*

After getting out of prison, I worked on the few magic tricks I knew whenever I could. One night I was sitting in a bar in Trenton watching a guy playing around with a deck of cards. I asked him if I could do a trick for him. He was impressed by the trick and wanted me to show him how I had done it. I shrugged, saying, "Yeah, I'll show you—for a drink." He said, "Why not?" After that I often used my magic to get free drinks.

In Belleville I picked up a few more trick things in a magic shop. And at the library I found some books on magic so I could learn more. I still couldn't read very well, but the illustrations always helped.

Another source of learning tricks was the shoe factory. Many of the workers at Bata Shoes had come to Canada from Hungary and Czechoslovakia, and they were into magic too. I became good friends with several of them, especially a lady from Budapest who taught me how to read tea leaves. She also taught me to read tarot cards and crystals.

Doing tricks in the bars for drinks was a blast. When a guy is half smashed anyway and he suddenly sees coins vanishing and then reappearing behind his ear, it's enough to almost blow his mind. One night I was having a good time trying a hanky trick that I had learned—making it change colors—and I noticed someone watching from across the room. He was of medium height and build, with a dark complexion—in his thirties, I guessed. He had a funny smile on his face, and then he moved to a table over near the TV set to get a better view of what I was doing. He just sat there, sipping a glass of beer and watching me, always with that smile.

It got late and I decided to head home. As I went out to the parking lot, I noticed that "Smiley" was following me. At first I thought maybe he was a cop trying to nail me for drinking under age. I knew I could get in trouble if the probation people found out I had been in a bar, so when the guy walked up and said, "Hey, you got a minute?" I was really tense and on my guard.

I stopped and said, "Well, I guess I've got a minute, but I've gotta get home—gotta get up and go to work in the morning."

"I was watching you back in the bar doing your tricks," he said with his easy smile. "You're pretty good, and you could be a lot better. I'm in a group that likes to do magic. In fact, we have real power—like you've probably never seen before."

That made me curious, and we talked for quite awhile. The guy's name was Jack, and finally he said, "Why don't you come on out to the farm and have a few drinks with us? It's just past Frankford . . . I'll show you some of my setup."

It was late, but I thought, *Why not?* So I followed him, driving past Frankford toward the tiny village of Stirling, about eight miles north. We pulled into a farmyard and parked. Inside he introduced me to his wife, Sonya, a pretty, dark-haired woman about his age. She had several friends who worked at Bata Shoes, including some people who worked right on my floor. She wanted to know where I had learned to do my tricks, and I told her, "In jail—I found this book and used to practice when I was doing time for robbery and murder."

I was testing them to see what they would think of having a jailbird in their home, but it didn't seem to bother them a bit. Later Jack asked me if I'd like to go downstairs to see his setup. As we went down the cellar steps, I noticed candles burning in little holders fastened to the walls. I thought that was odd—were they having trouble with their wiring?

Then we got to the door to the basement and went into a rather long, eerie, dimly lit room. A huge five-pointed star with a circle around it was painted on the floor. On the walls were odd pictures—an upside-down triangle and a goat with a huge horn coming out of the center of its head. Next to the pictures were strange, unintelligible words, and at one end of the room was a platform with a picture of a goat-headed man. Jack lit some more black candles, and I kept wondering, *Are they Catholics?*

Then he showed me some goblets and knives. As we talked he observed, "You know, I can tell when a person has power or wants power. You have a lot of resentment inside . . . you want to get revenge on someone, don't you?"

Surprised, I mumbled, "Yeah . . . how did you know?"

"I could tell . . . you know there are ways to do it without getting caught. Have you ever wanted to kill somebody . . . get rid of somebody . . . and not get caught?"

I was thinking, *Boy, this guy can read my mind.* Ever since my probation hearing, thoughts about how I could kill my father had never really left my mind.

Jack pressed me, saying, "Are you interested in knowing how to have power—and do better magic?"

"Sure," I said, and he and Sonya proceeded to demonstrate some of their repertoire. First, Jack used a trick that I later learned was called "the chick pan." He threw some powder into a big frying pan, dropped in a match, and covered it with a lid.

After a big flash and a puff of smoke, he took the lid off, and there was a live pigeon inside. That one impressed me, but he was just getting warmed up!

After having Sonya put her neck in a brace, he went through some incantations as if he were hypnotizing her. Taking a sword from a rack on the wall, he cut some newspaper into small strips to show me how sharp it was. Then, with a dramatic flourish, he put the sword into the brace around Sonya's neck and shoved it right through! It seemed to go right through her neck and out the other side! I gasped as he withdrew the sword, relieved to see there wasn't any blood on it. Sonya took off the brace and got up, perfectly in one piece. I knew it had been a trick, but he had done it so deftly I couldn't figure out how.

Well past midnight I finally said, "This has been great, and I'd like to know more. I'll be back sometime."

"Sure," Jack said. "Drop by anytime and we'll be glad to show you better stuff than this."

A few nights later I was back at the farm, drinking and playing cards with Jack and Sonya and some of their friends. After that I started going out to his farm almost every night for awhile to drink beer, talk, and learn more tricks. They asked me a lot of questions about how I'd gotten sent to reform school and what my family life had been like. That was all I needed, and I poured out my guts to them about my mom dying, my dad smashing me to bits, and his beatings when the cops would come.

They listened intently, nodding sympathetically, and seeming to understand just how I felt. I could feel their empathy for my bitterness and discovered that a lot of them were bitter too, about the government, about their supervisors at the shoe factory—about anybody in a position of authority.

One night they took me downstairs and had me put on a black sheet. Then they all did a weird dance in the center of the big five-pointed star with the circle around it. I just stood there and watched. The didn't offer any explanations, and I didn't ask any questions. On another night I joined in, doing the chanting and dancing, and I really got into it. We held hands and hopped around the pentagon together. They asked the spirits that I might be filled with "the power" and kept repeating the name "Beelzebub."

At first I thought they believed in old mythologies, something from the Greeks or Romans. Then I decided that they were gypsies because they were mostly Czechoslovakian or Hungarian in background, and all of them knew something about magic. They taught me a great deal about reading cards and crystals, and even palms.

But I figured it out slowly, because no one ever told me outright: they were witches, part of a group that worshiped Satan.

I kept going out there throughout the summer. Jack, Sonya, and the rest of them became my best friends—my special group to whom I could go for support. But I also needed interaction with people my own age, so I'd go to dances over at the Trenton High School, or at the air base nearby. Sometimes I dated girls I met at the shoe factory.

By Christmas I was promoted from the assembly line to the packing department where I'd put shoes, galoshes, and boots in boxes for shipment. It wasn't really that much better than sticking patches on running shoes, but it was different and the pay was better.

To supplement my salary, I constantly pilfered whatever I could from my fellow workers. During breaks I'd slip into the cloakroom and go through pockets for loose change. As I passed by workbenches, I'd pick up little items such as tools and buckles that I thought might be salable. I also took pieces of leather and pairs of shoes that had been rejected or damaged. I'd carry them out of the plant in a paper bag or sometimes just slip them under my jacket.

I sold what I stole wherever I could—in pawnshops, or to some guy who couldn't afford to buy shoes at a shoe store. The extra money helped, but if I wanted to be honest with myself, I would have probably stolen the stuff anyway. I liked the thrill of getting away with it, just as I had back in Sarnia when I was a little kid.

At the same time, I kept impressing my supervisors with my good work. Right after Christmas I decided to try to get into the Bata Shoe School of Design. I began to work my way up. I would fail written exams, but when it came to something visual, I could produce. I showed promise in drawing, creating, and copying.

Eventually I was promoted to the Design Department. Sometimes I was even sent out on the road to work as a sales clerk in some of the many shoe stores the Bata factory ran in the immediate area. Soon I was a main part of the Bata sales team in Ontario.

All the while I kept stealing and pilfering whatever I could. And once in the Design Department, I learned that I could take really nice shoe samples home without anybody asking any questions. Sometimes when out selling I would sneak shoes right off the store shelves, sell them on the sly, and pocket the money.

I was also stealing at home—from Mom and Dad Adams and from a Czechoslovakian lady named Helga, who rented a room upstairs next to mine. Helga had her money hidden under the bed in a suitcase, and I'd sneak in and take a few dollars now and then. I never took it all because that would have tipped her off. But by taking only a few bucks, she thought she couldn't remember where she spent it. She knew it was missing, but she couldn't prove anything.

I also kept drinking heavily on the sly and spending a lot of time out at the farm. Jack and his friends intrigued me and scared me at the same time. There was a lot of booze and taking pills, and sometimes we'd all wind up dancing around in the nude. I never bought into the witchcraft side of it too much, but sometimes I had to admit I sensed the presence of "someone" in the room. Once we went out to a cemetery, broke open a grave, and took the bones. I never quite understood why. Now I realize there *were* spirits there—evil ones.

By the fall of 1954 I was taken off probation. Mr. Cuthbertson came over to check on me for the last time and said, "You're doing great, LaVern—you're proving yourself. Keep it up! Remember," he said with a wink, *"you've got potential!"*

As soon as I was off probation, I decided I had had enough of the Adams and listening to all those hymns and all that Bible reading. I told them I was planning to move out. They looked sad, but they seemed to understand. Mrs. Adams said, "We'll pray for you, Son. We love you, and God loves you too. He's got plans for you, LaVern. Wait and see."

I didn't laugh in their faces—I respected them too much—but as I drove away I thought, *Forget it, you old bag! God has no plans for me!*

A new assignment with Bata Shoes worked in beautifully to get me completely away from Frankford. A job as a sales representative opened up in St. Catherine's, down at the southwest end of Lake Ontario, not far from Niagara Falls, around two hundred miles away. I found an apartment just outside St. Catherine's and began selling shoes in the area that fall.

I turned nineteen that October, and just before Christmas I was fired for stealing from the cash box in one of the stores where I worked. Getting fired didn't bother me too much. I was off probation and in no danger of having to go back to reform school. I knocked around for the next few months, working as a clerk in a clothing store and picking up other odd jobs. But by April I was running short of money and couldn't seem to hold down a job that paid much for very long.

I decided to contact a guy named Karl, whom I'd met almost a year before while having some drinks at a dance near Trenton. Karl had his own business—Famous Upholstery—in Belleville. I told Karl I needed a job, and he immediately offered one.

I moved back up to Belleville and found an apartment not too far from Famous Upholsterers. Karl taught me the upholstery business, and with my manual skills, I caught on quickly, learning to strip down the furniture and then recover it with new fabric.

I stayed on with Karl throughout the fall and winter. By the following spring, around Easter, Mrs. Adams learned I was back in the area. She phoned to ask me to come back and live with her and Clarence again. She also said she'd try to help me get my job back at Bata Shoes.

I was getting tired of upholstery—shoes were really my preference—so I agreed to move back in with the Adamses. She made a call to the shoe company and gave them her "please give him one more chance" speech. That carried a lot of weight because so many people in her family were connected to Bata.

I went back in and talked to one of the supervisors and told him that I was sorry about the pilfering. I said I'd done it only because I had been drinking heavily and had some gambling debts. "It won't happen again," I promised. "I've learned my lesson, and I really know that my future is in making shoes."

Somehow he bought my story and rehired me. I went back to work in the Bata Shoe School of Design and did very well. Of course, I went right back to pilfering sample shoes and anything else I could lay my hands on. By the following spring—April 1956—I graduated from the design school. A group of us decided to head over to Trenton for a big party with lots of drinking. A guy named Bob, who was my major competitor in the shoe school, challenged me to a chicken car race. By then I had a two-year-old Studebaker with overdrive, and many of us had recently seen a movie about hot-rodders in the United States playing chicken. We all went over to the Trent Canal Road, which was practically deserted at that time of night.

Bob took his car down about a quarter of a mile, while I waited in mine. Don, a guy who had served time with me in Bowmanville and also worked at the shoe factory, had decided to ride with me during the chicken race "just for kicks." When the signal was given, Bob and I hit our accelerators and roared straight at one another.

Bob must have been really drunk because he never "chickened." Just as I turned away, he caught the right front end of my car. The steering wheel was ripped from my grasp as our cars spun around in a splintering crash. In those days there were no seat belts, and Don went right through the windshield. He was killed instantly.

The police came, and Bob and I were charged with drunk driving. I lost my driver's license and also had to pay a five-hundred-dollar fine. No one was around to ask any questions or feel sorry for Don. He had no family, and when nobody claimed the body, it was buried in an unmarked grave in a Catholic cemetery just outside Trenton.

Luckily, I came through the crash with only minor cuts and bruises. Within a few days I was back at work in the shoe factory. My fellow workers whispered behind my back, "That's Powers for you—always getting drunk."

I didn't care what they said. I was just glad that I hadn't been seriously hurt and that the police hadn't figured out it had been a chicken race. With my record, that might have meant going back and doing more time—probably in Guelph. I tried to forget the wreck and Don's death, but guilt gnawed at me. Sometimes I'd have nightmares and relive the chicken race, waking up just before impact.

In May, just a few weeks after Don died, I went to a dance at the air base near Trenton with a girl named Sharon, who worked at Bata Shoes. Sharon had to take me in her car since mine was totaled, and I had no license anyway.

I didn't get home until early the next morning around six. I had drunk quite a bit, but I was able to negotiate the steps by the side door. I was about to slip up the stairs to my room when I glanced through the living room and into the kitchen. I spotted Mr. and Mrs. Adams, and I could see they were praying. I stopped to listen and heard them praying for their children. Then I heard my name mentioned.

I tiptoed back a few feet to where I could see and hear better as the Adams continued praying for their several grandchildren. I was about to turn and leave when Mrs. Adams started praying for me again: "Oh, Lord, please break our hearts and help us to love LaVern more and more . . . release him from his prison of hatred and bring him to yourself. . . ." Then she started to cry and almost gasped, "Oh, Lord, we love you . . . *we love you!*"

I was stunned by what I had heard, but I went upstairs, fell on the bed, and was asleep within minutes. I slept until midafternoon and finally got up and showered. I was really feeling rough, so I walked down to the Chinese restaurant a few blocks away and had a couple cups of coffee. After that, I wandered around town and wound up in Madill's—the biggest variety store in Frankford. Mr. Adams had been talking about replacing his little flashlight with a bigger one, and I knew Mrs. Adams needed some hooks and thread for her crocheting. So I bought both those items, plus some chocolate peppermints, because I knew they liked them.

When I got back to the house late in the afternoon with all my stuff, they were both there in the kitchen. They said hello but didn't mention my coming in at such a crazy hour. They had heard me leave earlier and wondered where I had gone and if everything was OK.

I looked at them sitting there and thought: *You're always concerned about me, always wondering what you could do to help me! Well, now I'm finally going to give something back to you!*

"Here!" I burst out, and I handed them my gifts. You would have thought it was Christmas the way they got so excited over that flashlight and the crocheting materials. And when Mrs. Adams saw the peppermints, she almost jumped up and down!

"I was wondering," I ventured, "if I could go to church with you tomorrow." Mom Adams flashed the biggest smile I'd ever seen on her face and came over to hug me. I hugged her back and hesitantly asked the really crucial question: "Would . . . would you mind if I call you Mom and Dad?"

She started crying and walked away a few feet. Finally she turned and said, "Of course, you can . . . Son."

About then I wanted to cry. I hadn't felt that much like crying for years, and I had to leave the room because I remembered my vow that I'd never cry again.

I went to church with them the next day at the Free Methodist church in Frankford. I was almost regretting my rash request, but I went because I said I would. At other times I had said I would go to church with them, but I had always broken my promise. This time I kept my word, and I sat through what seemed to be an awfully long sermon that didn't make much sense. For the next few weeks, I went to church with Mom and Dad Adams off and on. But I did it more to please them and not because I was getting a whole lot out of it.

When I had moved back up to Belleville from St. Catherine's, I had renewed my friendship with Jack and the rest of the coven up at Stirling. I still didn't put much stock in their witchcraft, but I hung around because I was curious. Besides, they were as friendly as ever and always treated me well. I was still interested in how to kill my father without getting caught, but I never learned much that I could really try. I did attempt to put a curse on him, but without some of his clothes or hair, they told me the curse probably wouldn't be effective.

Early that summer, I found new use for my connections to the coven. A beautiful blonde with a gorgeous figure came to work at Bata Shoes. The minute I saw her, I knew I wanted her. Gael was still in high school, trying to pick up some money in a summer job. I met her when she came to work in my department, and I soon learned that she knew the Adamses.

From the first day I met Gael, I tried everything I could to get a date. One of the women in the coven worked over in the leather department, and I asked her for help. She made me a potion and told me to slip it into a Coke and give it to Gael to drink. One day during break I had the doctored Coke all ready. But just as I tried to hand Gael the drink that would make her want me, some yo-yo bumped my arm and spilled the drink all over the place. I was mad enough to slug him, and I think I might have if Gael hadn't tried to distract me. "How are Mom and Dad Adams?" she asked as she cleaned up the spilled Coke. "I haven't seen them in church for the last two Sundays."

We got into a conversation about church, and I asked her,

"What do you get out of church? To me it's just a lot of mumbo-jumbo—and all they want is your money. The Bible is full of lies and fairy tales anyway."

I was giving her all the stuff I had heard all my life from Betty, but it didn't seem to bother Gael a bit. "It isn't just going to church, LaVern," she said. "It's knowing Jesus personally . . . knowing he died for my sins . . . that he cares about me and he goes with me everywhere." I stared at her and suddenly felt very sick to my stomach. I wound up having to excuse myself and went to the restroom to throw up.

The next time I was out at the coven I told them what had happened. Someone said, "She's a Christ-Christian . . . she has power, and she's dangerous. There's a real difference between Christ-Christians and church members. Some Christ-Christians have more power than we do."

I shrugged and tried to act unimpressed, but I began to wonder, *Is there really something to being a Christian?* I was also confused, because being around Mom and Dad Adams and all their praying and hymn singing had never made me ill. I decided it must be because they were older, sort of harmless, practically with one foot in the grave. But Gael was young and vibrant, and I couldn't deny how sick I had gotten the minute she told me about what being a Christian was really like.

Despite the warnings from my friends at the coven about "Christ-Christians," I continued trying to get a date with Gael. She was friendly, but she never gave me a tumble all summer long. I tried everything to get her to like me, including wearing a horrible-smelling pouch around my neck that a gypsy friend had provided, assuring me that it would make me totally desirable. I paid the gypsy fifty bucks for that pouch, but all it did was make me totally smelly.

When Gael left to go back to school that fall, I cursed my luck. Then I thought to myself, *Oh, well, there are plenty of other pretty little fish in the ocean. . . .*

Then one night the phone rang. It was Gael, wanting to know if we could go out.

"Why the sudden interest in me?" I wanted to know. "You didn't want to go out all summer. What's so special about now?"

"Oh, I wanted to go out," she assured me. "It was just that it wasn't the right time. How about this Saturday night?"

"OK," I said grudgingly, but my heart was pounding and the

blood was starting to race. We talked a while longer. Since I had finally gotten my driver's license back, I agreed to pick her up on Saturday at her home about twenty miles south of where I lived in Frankford.

After we hung up, I went out back of the house to light up a cigarette and to lay my plans. "She likes me after all . . . I've got to do this right . . . get some new clothes . . . some really good booze . . . first we'll go dancing, then we'll have a drink, and then . . . !" I smiled in the darkness and took another drag on my cigarette. At last things seemed to be going my way!

NINE

ANOTHER THIEF HEARS GOD SAY, "I LOVE YOU"

When I knocked on Gael's door that Saturday night, I was dressed to make a killing—$211 for a new sport coat, new shirt, cuff links, slacks, and a pair of $45 designer shoes I got at cost through the shoe company. And I had some very expensive booze in the trunk. By 1950s standards, I had spent a small fortune, but it would be worth it.

Meeting Gael's father made me nervous. He was a steel worker, but not the big burly type. Actually, he was thin and wiry, but his eyes seemed to bore right through me. Although he didn't say much, as we left he emphasized, "Make sure she's home by midnight."

I felt like saying, "What's going to happen? Is she going to turn into a pumpkin?" But I thought better of it, and Gael and I headed for Belleville. She had on a tight sweater and skirt, and her honey blonde hair curled down around her shoulders. She was an absolute knockout! This was going to be my night . . . I could feel it!

"Well, what shall we do first?" I asked. "Should we hit Tobe's for drinks, or should we go to the drive-in and then go over to Tobe's for some drinks and dancing afterward?"

Gael smiled that sweet smile and said, "No, we're going to the Masonic Temple."

"The Masonic Temple? There's no dance there on Saturday nights. They always have dances on Friday nights. . . ."

"Well, that's where we're going," is all Gael would say.

I decided to go along with her. Might as well humor her a little. You catch more flies with honey than vinegar anyway. I'd show her there wasn't much going on at the Masonic Temple, and then we could get on with the real fun of the evening.

As we turned the corner I could see a huge crowd filing into the Masonic Temple. The main parking lot was full, and I had to park almost a block away. As we walked toward the door, I noticed a lot of young people—couples and singles. There weren't many older people, and there wasn't any sign or anything to give me a clue as to what was going on. I'd been to the Temple several times before, but always for dances—maybe there was some special dance tonight?

I could hear music playing, stuff I couldn't recognize and when we got into the foyer a guy came up and sort of acted like an usher. He pointed us toward two seats down in front. Gael said, "We'll take them."

The moment we stepped into the main auditorium I smelled a rat, but I still couldn't quite figure out what was going on. The usher led us down front to the second row, and it was clear there wasn't going to be any dance that night. The place was packed with chairs, and up on the stage was an upright piano, a huge movie screen, and some kind of podium.

Just as I was asking Gael what was going on, a chubby guy ran up the aisle, grabbed a microphone, and boomed out, "Let's stand and sing, 'He Lives!'"

"Who died?" I asked Gael in a loud voice, and everybody around us seemed to gasp. She just laughed.

Next I heard the words *Youth for Christ.* "Youth for *who?*" I asked.

"Christ," said Gael.

"I think I want to get out of here."

"Please, LaVern, just wait awhile . . . "

What could I do? I was trapped, and if I wanted to keep the evening going with Gael, I had to stick it out.

Just then the chubby emcee, who was the local Youth for Christ director, Jim Blackwood, introduced a lanky guy who played the piano and told some really great jokes. Wes Arrum was big—really tall with blond hair—and I thought he had a fantastic sense of humor. His jokes were obviously very familiar to a lot of people sitting around us, but I'd never heard them before and I just roared. People kept turning around and looking at me as if to say, "Who *is* this guy? Hasn't he ever heard *these* before?"

Next came a local quartet, which sang several numbers. They were OK, nothing special, and then came the "quiz teams"—two groups of teenagers who competed with each other, answering questions about the Bible. I had never heard anything like it, and they really knew their stuff.

After the quiz teams came the evangelist who was going to be in town throughout the following week, speaking at the local high school auditorium. His name was Barry Moore. He told us that he had been a schoolteacher and was planning to become a missionary to France. Then he went into a little routine that featured an old joke about how the teacher went into the noisy classroom shouting, "Order, order, order!" and somebody hollered back, "I'll have fries and a Coke!"

I thought Barry Moore was pretty funny, too, almost as funny as Wes Arrum. It even crossed my mind, *I'd like to hear this guy speak.* Then he listed the titles of the talks he planned to give, and I was sure I wanted to hear him speak. On Monday night it would be "Booze Party in the Capital." Tuesday night would be, "Short Sheets and Narrow Covers." And Wednesday night's talk was supposed to be "What's in a Kiss?"

With titles like that, it can't be all boring, I thought to myself. *I think I'll see if Gael wants to go.* The evening ended with the showing of the film, "Seventeen." That was a real downer because it included a scene where a guy got killed in a chicken car race. It was all like a huge flashback to the night when Don died, and it took the edge off of the evening for me. Still, I was really impressed with all the enthusiasm and the way the quiz team popped up to answer questions before the guy had even finished asking them. And with all the young people there my age, the evening seemed to be something very, very real.

Feeling kind of subdued, I didn't suggest to Gael that we go drinking and dancing. I just took her home, but I did remember to ask her if she wanted to go hear Barry Moore preach the following Monday. She said of course she did and went on into the house. As I got back in the car, I noted with some satisfaction that I'd gotten her in by eleven-thirty, well ahead of her dad's midnight deadline.

Gael called me on Sunday night to remind me that I had promised to take her to Barry Moore's meeting on Monday.

"Yeah, yeah, I'm taking you," I said. "I'll pick you up at six-thirty."

Quickly I dialed Wayne and Ross, a couple of guys who worked with me at Bata Shoes, and told them about Barry Moore and the meeting. "You'll get a bang out of this," I said. "It'll be good for laughs. Why don't you come along with us?" They agreed to go along.

The next night I wound up with everybody in my car, headed for the local high school. By then I'd had time to think it over a little—and I didn't really feel like going, but I was cornered. I'd invited my buddies and couldn't back out now.

We all went in and sat about halfway down. Wayne, Ross, and I spent most of the evening goofing around, making fun of the preacher and lead singer, and embarrassing Gael no end. But when Barry Moore gave his invitation, Wayne and Ross went forward! I thought it was a joke—that they were trying to put me on—but it wasn't a joke at all. They were serious!

I had to hang around while they had counseling, and then I took everybody home. We drove to Gael's place first, and I could hear them talking quietly to her about what had happened. She didn't say much, but she was very supportive of what they had done. When I dropped her off I said, "I'll pick you up tomorrow night, and I won't have these guys along."

She looked at me, sort of surprised, and then said, "Well, sure, I'll be ready by six-thirty."

On the way back up to Frankford, Wayne and Ross started trying to witness to me and share what had happened to them. I told them to knock it off—that I didn't want to hear it and that they had made fools of themselves. And if they wanted to go to tomorrow night's meeting, they would have to find their own way!

The next night I drove over to Gael's house with all that booze still in the trunk of the car. I wondered if we'd ever get to drink any of it and if I'd ever get to first base with Gael. Come to think of it, I'd never even gotten into the batter's box! At the same time, I wondered what I was doing, going back to hear this stupid preacher for a second time.

Barry Moore's text that night was from Luke 23:39-43, which talks of the two thieves who were crucified with Christ, one on his left and the other on his right. As one of the thieves hung there in pain, he hurled insults at Jesus. "If thou be Christ, save thyself and us." But the other thief rebuked his partner, saying,

"Dost not thou fear God, seeing thou art in the same condemnation? And we indeed justly; for we receive the due reward of our deeds: but this man hath done nothing amiss." Then the second thief turned to Christ and said, "Lord, remember me when thou comest into thy kingdom." Jesus answered, "Verily I say unto thee, Today shalt thou be with me in paradise."

After reading the Scripture text, Barry Moore really got into his talk. He had a flamboyant, dramatic style, crouching low, holding his big Bible in one hand as he stabbed the air with his index finger.

Then I heard him saying, "You know what it's like to *lie*, don't you? You know what it's like to *steal*, don't you?" I began to feel very guilty and uncomfortable. I wanted to be with Gael, but I didn't want to be hearing *this*. Anger burned inside, and I thought, *Who needs it? I'd just as soon go to Tobe's—anywhere, as long as it's out of this place.*

I made motions to Gael that I'd like to leave, but she kept her eyes intently on Barry Moore. He kept shaking that finger, and even though we were sitting well toward the back of the room, I swore that he was pointing right at me. I couldn't take it any longer! I jumped up, ready to leave. Gael looked at me but wouldn't get up. I snarled, "You dumb little . . . if you can tell him all about me, he can give you a ride home!"

Gael looked at me as if I were crazy and gasped, "What are you talking about?"

"Never mind—both of you can go . . . !" I wanted to hit her, but instead I spun around and tore out of there, jumped in my car, and burned rubber all the way out of the parking lot. I remembered the booze I still had in the trunk, and I headed for Stirling where I hoped to find some drinking buddies from my coven. No such luck—no one was around anywhere. I headed back to Frankford, driving around for what seemed like hours.

I never did stop to take a drink. Instead I spent the time arguing and swearing at Someone I didn't even know existed. I told God off, screaming and shouting and cursing, but all it got me was exhaustion. I finally pulled up by the Trent Canal in Frankford and sat there for a long time, looking at the water rolling lazily by.

The thought crossed my mind, *Why not take the spare tire out of the trunk, tie it around your neck, and jump in?* I wanted to die, but I was too afraid. I pulled away from the edge of the canal and kept driving. Around 1:30 in the morning I went back to the Adamses' place and dragged myself upstairs to my back bedroom, feeling spent and totally miserable.

I sat on my bed and gazed out the window that had a view of the hill in back of the Adamses' property. It was Wednesday morning, October 3, 1956, and as I gazed at that hill, I noticed two power poles at the top that looked like crosses etched against a full October moon. The scene brought back Barry Moore's text about how Jesus and the thieves had been nailed to crosses on a hill outside Jerusalem.

Then I got angry again—with Gael, with Barry Moore, and especially with God. I started muttering and then talking loudly. "Stupid woman, just forget this thing . . . forget it . . . !" I pulled a cigarette out of my jacket and tried to light it, but threw it away when I discovered the wrong end in my mouth. I had lit the cork tip instead!

I lit another cigarette and, almost shouting, continued to argue with God: "What have you ever done for me? You killed my mother and Kathleen's little boy. You let my father beat me and practically kill me. Why should I love you? Why? Why? *Why?*"

I stopped to take a long drag on my cigarette, and then I heard a voice! *"Because I sent my Son to die for you."*

It sounded like Barry Moore's voice, but Barry Moore wasn't there. I called out, "Mrs. Adams?" There was no answer. Then I looked in the bathroom—nothing there. I looked under the bed and in the closet, but there was no one anywhere! Then I started to shake. *You're going over the edge, just like your aunt. . . .*

I was remembering one of Betty's sisters who had become an alcoholic and started to hear things. She started to talk to herself and they put her away. And now I was hearing voices too! What had the high priest of the coven said? "Keep away from those Christ-Christians because they're dangerous— *they've got more power than all of us put together.*"

Then I said aloud, "OK, you sent your Son, Jesus. Why? You can't answer me, can you? Why?"

The voice said, *"Because I love you!"*

"Nobody loves me!" I almost screamed the words through clenched teeth.

"I love you . . . I love you."

Then I remembered Barry Moore's sermon—how Jesus

turned to the thief and lovingly said, "Today you will be with me in paradise."

At that instant, all of the hurt and pain of thirteen years that had been held inside welled up in my throat. *Oh, God, no, I'm going to cry . . . I'm going to cry . . . but real men don't cry, babies cry!* I was twenty years old, with my twenty-first birthday just three weeks away. Officially, I would be a man, yet here I was, overwhelmed by the need to cry.

I couldn't hold it any longer. I fell to the floor and began to cry. I wept and wept and continued to weep. It was like a dam had burst inside, and the tears poured out of me. I kept moaning, "Forgive me, forgive me . . . I'm sorry, I'm sorry . . . ."

I don't know how long I cried—it seemed like an hour. I was tired, so very tired. My eyes hurt, in fact, I hurt all over, and I knew I had to sleep. I crawled, clothes and all, into bed and lay there, still crying and whimpering. I cried aloud for my mother—not Betty, but my real mother. "Oh, Mum, Mum, why did you leave me?"

And I could hear her sweetly say, *"There you are, Laddie, so you want to ride the horsie?"*

My shrill, childish voice answered, *"Oh, yes, yes, bouncer, bouncer!"*

At last I drifted off to sleep as the full moon moved on past the hill in back of the house and the two "crosses" faded into blackness. Almost two thousand years before two thieves had been given the opportunity to know God's love. One had accepted it, the other had not. And now another thief had made his choice. He, too, could look forward to paradise.

TEN

"WHAT'S HAPPENED TO YOU, POWERS?"

Less than three hours later, out of habit, I awoke at 6:30 and realized I had to go to work. Somehow it was easy to get out of bed. When I looked at the face in the mirror as I shaved, it didn't look like the guy from the day before. This person looking back at me out of the mirror was different.

I found myself humming, feeling good—no, actually, almost giddy or silly. Despite so little sleep, I didn't even feel tired. I practically bounced down the stairs, and there were Mom and Dad Adams, sitting down to have breakfast.

"Hi, Dad, how are you doing? Hi, Mom . . . boy that smells good."

They both looked up in surprise. Those weren't my usual greetings because I never liked getting up much. And now there was a new sound in my voice they'd never heard before.

Dad Adams chuckled, "Oh, oh, something's happened. There's a guy in love here. Did somebody get engaged?"

He knew I had been dating Gael, and I guess he thought we'd fallen in love. But Mom said, "Oh . . . no . . . I know what it is!"

I looked at her with a big smile on my face.

"Yes, you've received Jesus, haven't you, Son?"

I put my head down . . . the tears were starting to come again . . . and Mom almost shouted, "Praise the Lord!"

I jumped off my chair, and we both started crying and hugging each other. I lifted her right off the floor! Then I hugged Dad, too, but with his three hundred pounds I had to be content to hug him where he sat.

I don't remember what happened to breakfast, but I do know I never ate anything. We prayed together, we read the Bible together, and we hugged some more. I felt great—I really did! We all chose a card from the Promise Box on the table, and I picked Jeremiah 33:3: "Call unto me and I will answer thee and shew thee great and mighty things, which thou knowest not." At that moment I had no idea how prophetic those words would be for me.

Dad Adams was the first to pray, and I couldn't help it—I started to cry and couldn't stop. Then Mom prayed and started crying, too. Dad Adams reached out and put his giant hand on my shoulder, saying, "Jesus, here is your child."

Then it was my turn to pray, and all I could say was, "Thank you for whatever is happening."

Before I headed for work, I asked them to forgive me for so many things—being a jerk, pilfering, and making fun of them behind their backs.

"Never mind, it's taken care of. We love you," they said. Dad Adams put his big paw on my shoulder again and said, "Welcome to the family, Son."

I finally grabbed my lunch and headed for work. Driving along the Trent Canal about two miles from the factory, I remembered all that liquor in the back of the car. I hit the brakes, backed up a little and found a narrow road that took me right down to the edge of the canal.

I was happy, actually laughing. As I opened the trunk, I said aloud, "Well, I don't need *this* any more." I grabbed the bottles of liquor—expensive stuff that I'd bought for my big date with Gael—and smashed them on the rocks. I got sort of carried away and smashed everything I could find, including several bottles of Coke. I couldn't care less . . . I was feeling giddy and silly.

When I got to work, the feeling hadn't worn off. I said hi to everybody on the way in, and they looked at me in shock. Powers had never greeted anyone before. I got upstairs, put on my smock, and got my machine going. People kept coming in, and I kept calling out, "Hi, how are you doing this morning?"

They just stared at me and then hurried by, wanting to get away as quickly as possible. After I got the conveyor belt going, I went over to help somebody else, but all he did was pull his hands back and say, "Get away from me . . . what's the matter with you . . . what's happened to you, Powers?"

I couldn't figure it out at first, but later it occurred to me that I was a mess! When I had smashed all the booze on the rocks, some of it had splashed on my clothes. So there I was at work, smelling like booze, my eyes red from lack of sleep, with a silly grin on my face, acting a little bit out of my mind. Everyone there was sure I was drunk. They were scared to death I'd hurt someone, especially with all that machinery running.

At 9:15 the conveyor stopped for break time. I was sitting there still feeling good when the floor supervisor, Tio Kravacheck, a big burly Czechoslovakian, loomed over me. "Powers, we've got complaints against you that you're drunk and endangering the lives of these people."

Laughing, I said, "Tio, I'm not drunk. I haven't even been drinking."

Tio looked doubtful, and so did the people who had crowded in behind him. LaVern Powers claiming he hadn't been drinking! I had so often come to work with a hangover, feeling hostile, but I would usually stay to myself and not bother anybody. This morning, however, I was laughing, giddy, and acting a little crazy.

Tio and I kept arguing about how drunk I was or wasn't, and he kept pushing me toward the doors. He wanted to get me out of there. People could see that Tio was angry, and a bigger crowd kept gathering. But I just kept laughing, saying, "C'mon, Tio, lay off . . . I'm fine. It's just because I'm happy. There's nothing wrong with me."

I really wasn't prepared to say I was a Christian because I didn't understand what had happened to me. Tio didn't know what to do with me. He smelled the booze on my clothes and saw that I was acting weird. Finally, he said exasperatedly, "You better tell me what's going on here, Powers, or you're finished. You've already gotten one break. This could ruin you. Don't ruin your life."

"No, Tio," I responded. "I'm not ruining anything."

"Just think of something," he hissed, trying to keep his voice down. "Just be sick or something."

"Well, why should I, Tio? . . . I'm not sick . . . it's hard to explain."

"Well, then, tell me, c'mon . . . tell me what's going on."

I tried to mumble something, but he grabbed my shoulder

and said, "Look me in the face and say what you're going to say."

And so I looked him right in the eye and said loudly, "This morning I prayed and asked Jesus to come into my life and forgive me."

The crowd of workers who had gathered around were stunned for a second. Then the laughing started. At the same time, Tio—this big burly Czechoslovakian who had been gripping my shoulder—suddenly had his huge arms around me saying, "Hello, brother!"

It turned out Tio was a member of the local Pentecostal church. All I could say was, "Yeah? Yeah? You, too?" The whole floor seemed to be laughing, but Tio ignored them. "I understand, I understand," he told me. "We'll go for coffee . . . let's go for coffee."

As we went out the side door, somebody hollered, "Fire the dumb jerk!" and there was more laughing.

Tio and I went over to a lounge to have coffee, and he wanted to hear exactly what had happened. I told him about dating Gael, going to the Barry Moore meetings, and what had happened during the night in my room. Then I told him about smashing the bottles of booze against the rocks on the way to work and how happy I had been feeling ever since I had gotten up.

Tio took a sip of coffee and asked, "Well, who counseled you?"

"Why . . . nobody did, I guess. I was just there in my room and I knew God loved me. . . ."

"Just you? Nobody else? You should go back to that revival meeting . . . you should go back and talk to that minister and get some help."

"Yeah, OK, Tio, I'll do that . . . I'll do that."

We finished our coffee and I went back to work. I was still feeling great even though all day people just snickered and laughed behind my back or right in my face. But I didn't care, I really didn't. At lunch hour I went out to the cafeteria to get something to eat. When I finished lunch I had my usual cigarette. A couple of guys walked up and said, "Hey, Powers, don't you know Christians don't smoke?"

"No, I didn't know. What's that got to do with being Christian?"

They just laughed and walked away.

I had a lot to learn about Christian taboos and what people

thought Christians did or didn't do. I didn't quit smoking for almost a year after I became a believer, but I stopped drinking immediately, even though I was a borderline alcoholic. Something told me that booze had been in control and now God had to be in charge. I had known alcohol was destroying me, but becoming a Christian made the difference. I never craved another drink.

I got off work at 4:30 and hurried home to shower, clean up, and grab a quick bite of supper before going over to Belleville, where Barry Moore was holding his meetings. I wanted to get there early so I could talk to him before anyone else arrived, and I was on the front steps when the caretaker opened the door. Barry came in a few minutes later with Jim Blackwood, the Belleville YFC director. I stopped Barry and asked if I could talk to him.

The evangelist was wary at first because he thought we were going to have some kind of confrontation. He recognized me from the night before—the crazy young guy who had jumped up and dashed out in the middle of the meeting. But when I introduced myself and told him I needed some help, he relaxed and asked me to share just what had happened.

We sat down together, and he opened the Bible and asked me to read various verses. I stumbled over a lot of the words and finally he said, "You're having a hard time."

"Yeah, I don't read too well . . . I hardly have any education."

"But you told me you have an important position at the Bata Shoe Company?"

"Yeah, I do, but I still have a hard time reading. My writing is pretty good, and when you show me something I can do it, but I don't read very well."

Barry nodded sympathetically and went slower after that. He kept asking, "Do you understand?"

"Yeah, I think so. You explain the big words, and I think I can tell what it means."

Barry took me through what he called the "Romans Route of Salvation," going first to Romans 3:23: "For all have sinned, and come short of the glory of God."

"Do you recognize that you're a sinner?" he asked.

"I do now, but all I could have told you before was that I'm an ex-con."

"What do you mean?"

"I've served time—in reform school. I've robbed people and was involved in the death of an old carny lady."

"Oh, really . . . ," said Barry. "But do you understand that you're a sinner?"

"Yes, I understand—it's what I've done wrong. It's my stealing, cheating, and lying . . ."

"No, that's not quite it," he corrected me. "It's not just your lying and stealing—that's just part of it. The real trouble is your rejection of God and his Son." And then he turned to Romans 6:23: "For the wages of sin is death; but the gift of God is eternal life through Jesus Christ our Lord."

"You know what wages are, don't you?" Barry asked me.

"That's what you earn," I replied.

"That's right, and what you've done against God has earned you the death penalty. It's due, and you're supposed to pay, but now you don't have to. God has paid the penalty and given you the gift of eternal life. You've had a hard life, and God won't change what happened. But despite all your sins, he's willing to change what will happen from here on out. He has paid the highest price so that you can have his free gift. All you have to do is receive his Son. Do you believe that?"

What had happened to me in my room the night before was becoming clearer. I looked right back at Barry and said, "Yes."

Then he turned to Romans 10:9-10: "That if thou shalt confess with thy mouth the Lord Jesus, and shalt believe in thine heart that God hath raised him from the dead, thou shalt be saved. For with the heart man believeth unto righteousness; and with the mouth confession is made unto salvation."

"Now listen to this, LaVern, what you did this morning at the factory when you were talking to your supervisor in front of all those people—that's confessing with your mouth. But the believing in your heart is what I want to talk about. Do you know where your heart is?"

"Yeah, here," I answered, tapping my chest.

"That thing in your chest can be replaced," Barry said, poking me in the chest with his finger, "but this can't." He reached up and tapped the side of his head.

His finger stabbed out again into my chest. "Remember, *this* can be replaced, but *this* . . ."—and he tapped me gently on the temple—"this is where you think. This is where you really believe. Do you understand?"

I didn't.

Barry pressed on with intensity in his voice. "I've got news for you, LaVern, and you've got to believe this. You've got to believe God's Word because it's going to be a fight every day of your life. Sin doesn't want to let you go that easily. You've got to *think* . . . *that's* how to believe in your heart that God has saved you."

And then we turned to John 3:16. As Barry read the verse, he inserted my name: "For God so loved LaVern that he gave his only begotten Son, that if LaVern believeth in him, LaVern should not perish, but have everlasting life."

God so loved LaVern! Barry's words stuck in my mind and kept repeating themselves over and over. I felt those same feelings surging up in my chest, and I wanted to cry. I realized again that Somebody really did love me. All my life I had never heard the words, "I love you," not even from my mother. She did love me, of course, but she had never used those words—it just wasn't her way. And everything my father had done had communicated exactly the opposite.

Mom and Dad Adams had said they loved me, but it didn't register the way it was registering now. I always thought that the Adamses meant they *liked* me. When they said, "We love you, Son," I'd just say to myself, "Yeah . . . yeah . . . you say you love me, but you can't because you aren't my parents and you don't really know me."

To tell the truth, I really didn't even know what real love was because I felt I had never been loved. All the horror and hatred that filled my life at age seven must have blocked out the early years of being touched by my mother and hearing her tender brogue saying, "You're my little baron. You're mine, Lad . . . you'll always be mine!"

My years in the gang and in reform school had taught me to understand the word *love* in cheap and shallow terms: I loved candy, I loved chocolate, I loved money, or I loved a girl for sexual satisfaction. But long ago when a tiny boy had played "ride the horsie" on his mother's back, using her braided hair for reins, seeds of love had been planted that were never fully lost. They were stifled and left dormant for years, but at that crucial moment in my room, everything had changed. When I cried that night for the first time in thirteen years, it was then that I realized Somebody did care about me after all. Somebody actually wanted *me!*

Nothing I could do could return the want that God had for me because his giving would always outdo anything I could give back. I could never outgive the God who wanted me so desperately to be his that he gave his most precious possession, his Son.

God had exchanged his Son for me and I was *wanted.* I realized that the One who had created everything, this God who could destroy the world, this God who I had always been told was hatred and judgment, vindictive and cruel, was *none* of those things. He was *love.* When Barry put my name in John 3:16, I was overwhelmed. The tears came in torrents, and I wept without shame as the meeting was about to start.

ELEVEN
"YOU KNOW THAT YOU KNOW THAT YOU KNOW!"

Barry Moore waited patiently as I wept. The choir was finishing some opening hymns and he would have to speak in a few minutes, but he didn't leave just yet.

I couldn't be sure, but maybe he was embarrassed by tears from a guy twenty years old. Barry didn't really know me then. We would become better acquainted over the next few years, and I would learn that Barry was much less emotional than I. When he told me, "Your heart is up *here,*" he had tapped on his head. For Barry, believing meant understanding Scriptures and then putting your faith in what God promised.

But for me, Christianity has always been something I've felt deep inside. I understand, I believe—but I *feel* God's love in a way that is very personal and very real. The little boy who vowed not to cry and didn't for thirteen years now cries easily as a man. It's not that I'm using tears to flush out tensions or other emotions. In fact, sometimes I feel uncomfortable with tears, especially when it happens on a platform where I am speaking or performing. I fight the tears then because some groups don't consider weeping very proper, as if it points to some kind of weakness or lack of faith. But when I fight tears, I know I'm fighting the Holy Spirit.

Over the years I've always been emotional with my family, shedding tears easily to let them know how I feel about them. I explain that before I came to Christ I had been so alone and so afraid. It's a terrible tragedy to let absolute loneliness consume you before you can ever discover life. I thank God I discovered him (actually, he found *me*) before the loneliness ate me alive. And once God broke through the hard and brittle shell I had built around myself, the tears flowed easily.

I can't stop the tears any more than I can stop the rain because I know God loves me. As I've often told my daughters, Tina and Paula, when God comes into your life, *you know that you know that you know!* You know that you're loved, and you know that you know it. You just know it—you have no doubts!

But I didn't have all this worked out on that night back in 1956, as I sat with Barry Moore, the evangelist, out behind a platform in a high school gym in Belleville, Ontario. Barry waited until I could control myself, and then he showed me one more verse. It was John 1:12: "But as many as received him, to them gave he power to become the sons of God, even to them that believe on his name."

"Have you received him, LaVern?" Barry asked.

"Yes, oh yes, I have!"

"Well, Buddy, all I can tell you is, according to the Scriptures, you're part of the family. And all I can say is, welcome to the family! I have to go, but I'll see you later."

Those were the same words that Dad Adams had used that morning. I thought he was welcoming me to his own family in a new and different way because now I believed what he believed, but when Barry Moore said it, the full meaning struck home. *Now I was part of God's family,* and I knew that I knew that I knew it was true!

Life changed for me in many ways after the Barry Moore Crusades. For one thing, I changed my name to Paul by the following Saturday night when I attended a YFC "Funspiration." I still didn't know anything about the apostle Paul. I hadn't even had time to read about him yet in the Bible. But I'd always hated the name LaVern, and I'd always liked the name Paul. Now, after being born again, it seemed a good time to make a switch, so I started asking people who knew me to call me by my new name. And when I met anyone for the first time, I introduced myself as Paul Powers.

I also changed my recreational habits. Instead of going out to drink and dance on Saturday nights, I spent them in the front row of Youth for Christ rallies. I told Jim Blackwood, the local director, that I wanted to help, so he let me pass out songbooks, set up chairs, and run the film projector. I took my jobs seriously, actually thinking these duties were more important than what I was doing down at the shoe factory, where I had risen to a manager's status and had about one hundred people working under me.

I also quit the witches' coven. When word got around about my conversion, one of the coven members slipped up to me at work and let me know, "You better not talk about us . . . you'd better be careful what you say. . . ."

My only response was, "Why would I want to talk about you? I've got other things going with my life."

Along with rejecting witchcraft, I stopped doing magic tricks, especially with decks of cards. I threw out all my tarot cards and the crystal ball and crystals that I had gotten from friends in the coven. I'd been working hard on concentration with the crystal ball, which was used for "seeing" and contacting evil spirits. Basically, I just quit doing all tricks—cigarette tricks, hanky tricks, coin tricks—they all had to go because I associated them with an old life that I wanted to have no part of again.

Another thing that had to go was my hatred for my father. A couple of weeks after I received Christ, a YFC counselor took me aside one Saturday night and talked to me about my resentment and hatred. He knew quite a bit about my background, and he talked with me about this problem of being bitter toward my father. He wanted to know if I had notified my family, and I said, "No, I hate my parents." Then he really dealt with me from the Scriptures, and I was embarrassed. I told him I would pray and ask God to help me forgive them.

Mom Adams also urged me to call my family and try to reestablish contact. I decided I didn't hate my father that much, but I didn't really love him either. I would have changed my last name along with my first if I could have figured out how to do it. But finally I agreed to make the call. Betty answered, and the moment she heard my voice she slammed down the phone. I tried again, and she hung up again. I tried a third time, and went through the operator with a person-to-person call to Albert Powers. My father came on the line, and I blurted out, "This is LaVern. I just want to say I'm going to church now and I don't hate you."

My father laughed—a short, bitter little laugh—and said, "I don't have any more money and I don't have any more time," and he hung up. Next I wrote letters trying to explain what had happened to me. I didn't want his money; I wanted to tell him about Christ and salvation from sin.

I tried my best to share my testimony, but I'm afraid I said things in my letters that blamed and condemned him and Betty. God had changed me and taken me out of all that, and I really wanted them to know what had happened. I didn't want them to go to hell, but I let them know that that's where they were headed. I quoted from gospel tracts and from Bible verses that spoke of condemnation for unbelievers.

I asked people I knew to pray for my dad and Betty, and I kept sending letters. After about the third or fourth letter, they started coming back unopened and labeled, "Return to sender." Then a Christmas card I sent came back. I began writing with a softer tone, but all the letters came back unopened. Whenever I heard of a preacher in Sarnia or of an evangelist who would be speaking in that area, I asked them to look my parents up. I'm sure some of them did, but it didn't do any good.

Something I did keep was my relationship with Gael. A few nights after the Barry Moore Crusades I called her and apologized for the way I had acted. We got back together and dated steadily for the next year or so. From then on, however, I was a complete gentleman—no more scheming to get her drunk so I could seduce her. We went regularly to Youth for Christ rallies every other Saturday night, and for a long time I thought one day I would marry her.

My new life as a Christian soon brought me face to face with one of my major needs—to learn to read well. As I tried to read the Bible, I struggled and made little headway. Having devotions was discouraging, and I knew I had to do something. After the first of the year, I enrolled in a public night school, hoping to finish my education. My teacher was Miss Sandenburg, an old lady who wore her silver-grey hair in a bun. She had glasses, always wore dark dresses, and her skin was as wrinkled as Mrs. Adams's.

On the first night of classes she said, "Now I want all of you new Canadians who are taking this English class to tell me something about yourselves." Here I was, already a Canadian in this class filled with Japanese, Chinese, Czechoslovakians, and Hungarians who were all anxious to learn to read so they could become citizens of Canada. Miss Sandenburg asked each of us to get up and give our names, where we lived, what country we were from, and what we hoped to learn in the class.

When my turn came, I rose to my feet and said, "My name is Paul Powers. I'm from Frankford, Ontario. I work at the Bata Shoe Company, and I want to learn to read."

Miss Sandenburg stared at me and said, "What?"

"I want to learn to read," I replied. "I am not stupid."

"I didn't say you were, young man," was her tart reply.

"Well, I've been told all of my life I am stupid, that I am dumb, and I am not."

Miss Sandenburg just looked back at me, not smiling, but obviously wondering how this character had found his way into her class. Later, as she was going around looking at everyone's handwriting, she stopped and said, "I want to talk with you when class is over. I think I know you."

After class I came up to her and she said, "You go to Bethel Chapel, don't you?"

"Yeah, that's my church."

Miss Sandenburg told me she was a member at Bethel and added, "Do you really want to learn to read?" I told her I certainly did, and she said, "Well, you don't need this," pointing to the regular class textbook. "That's not the book you want."

"Oh, what book do I want then?"

"You want a Bible . . . you'll want to use your Bible—that's your best textbook."

"Well, Mr. Moore gave me a Bible. It has the Old and New Testament, and it's a pretty big book."

Miss Sandenburg nodded with approval and started me out in the Gospel of John in the New Testament. Whenever I was called on to read in class, I was to read from the Bible.

She also spent a lot of time giving me private tutoring. I would read along with her, and she would challenge me to understand what I was reading.

When my Youth for Christ friends heard I was really learning to read and understand the Bible, they tried to help too. I'd read passages to them, and they'd ask me if I understood what they meant. I had started going to Bethel Chapel because two of the ushers from Youth for Christ went there, as did Jim Blackwood, the YFC director. My usual plan was to come into Belleville for a rally on Saturday night, then stay overnight with friends and go to church with Jim and the others.

On every other weekend, however, when rallies weren't being held, I would go to church with Mom and Dad Adams, who alternated between the Nazarene church in Trenton and the Free Methodist church in Frankford. Later I started going along with Jim Blackwood to help him conduct rallies in towns throughout outlying areas, to the north and east of Belleville.

Jim's responsibilities covered a radius of some one hundred miles, and we went everywhere to show Billy Graham films, especially the one about Jim Vaus called *Wire Tapper.* I kept track, and during that period we showed *Wire Tapper* 119 times. I loved to hear Evangeline Carmichael sing during that film: "I cannot hide from God, however I may try. Though mountains cover me, I'll not escape his eye." I loved those words. I still love them today. As a new convert, I'd hear her sing as we showed the film, and I'd say, "Yeah, that's me, that's *me!*"

As I started learning to read better, I got involved with the Bible quiz team from Belleville. During the summer of 1957 our Belleville Bible quiz team became champion of Eastern Canada and was invited to compete in international competition at Winona Lake, Indiana, in July. The timing was perfect because Bata Shoes always shut down every July and August due to the incredible humidity, which made it impossible to work in a factory that specialized in vulcanizing processes that generated tremendous heat. With no air conditioning, it simply became unbearable to work.

I drove down with the quiz team to help cheer them on. I also did what I could by drilling different members on their questions and being chief gofer for the entire group. The Bible quiz competition was held in the huge Billy Sunday Tabernacle at Winona Lake, and one night Bob Pierce, founder of World Vision, spoke on the topic, "What on Earth Are You Doing for Christ's Sake?" His title was guaranteed to get a lot of double takes because it almost sounded like blasphemy, but Dr. Pierce was totally serious about the question his startling phrase posed.

In a quiet, nonshouting way, he challenged thousands of us to take inventory on what we were doing on this earth for the sake of Jesus Christ. His message was a milestone in my spiritual life. I came home knowing I wanted to go into full-time ministry for Christ—someday, somewhere. I was on this earth to do something for Jesus' sake, and I had no choice but to follow him.

I spent the rest of the summer traveling with Jim Blackwood throughout Ontario, Quebec, and the Maritime provinces, showing films and raising money for World Vision. This became a regular summer routine with me, which I would follow for several years.

I kept dating Gael throughout the rest of 1957, but just before Christmas we both realized that our relationship was not destined to become permanent, and so we parted on friendly terms.

When the shoe factory reopened that fall, I also went back for a second session in night school with Miss Sandenberg. On the first night she said, "Paul, I think it's time for you to start using a different book to practice your reading—try this."

She handed me a copy of *Pilgrim's Progress* by John Bunyan. I was soon enthralled by Bunyan's world of fantasy and allegory. Bunyan was a master storyteller, and I started using him for a model whenever I went out speaking for YFC.

Youth for Christ continued to be the center of my social and spiritual life. Some of the greatest Christian speakers of the day appeared at the YFC Saturday night rallies, including Jack Wyrtzen; Dr. Oswald J. Smith, founder of the Missionary Church in Toronto; Jack Hamilton; Ted Engstrom; Bob Cook; and a western movie star named Redd Harper, who toured Ontario in the spring of 1958.

I had met Redd before but under much different circum-stances. I knew Redd wouldn't remember me, but the night he talked in Belleville I went up afterward and got in line with a group of teenagers who wanted him to sign their Bibles. There I was, almost twenty-two years old, but I wasn't embarrassed. I stepped up and said, "Would you sign this for me, Mr. Harper?"

"Sure, padnah," and he scribbled his name with a flourish.

As he handed my Bible back to me, I said, "We've met before."

"Oh?"

"Yes . . . I've seen both of your movies—*Mr. Texas* and *Oiltown, U.S.A.*"

"Yes, well, Youth for Christ uses them a lot, I guess . . . " He was puzzled, wondering what I had meant by saying we had met before.

"Yes, but when I saw you it wasn't at a YFC rally, it was up near Oshawa."

A glimmer of recognition came into Redd's eye. "Oh, yeah, I was there with Gus Ambrose quite awhile back."

"Right—1952—and you showed *Mr. Texas* and gave your testimony."

"Yeah, I remember . . . we had some good meetin's in those days. Singin' about our Lord."

"Yeah, I was the projectionist in the Bowmanville reform school when you came through."

Redd's eyes got a little bigger. "You were *what?*"

"Yes, you came up and thanked me afterward. I was upstairs in the little projection booth rewinding the film. You wanted to make sure that it was clean—that I was using a clean piece of tissue. You thanked me for keeping it clean because it was your own personal print."

"Oh yeah! You that kid?"

"Yes."

"What are you doing here?"

"I became a Christian about two years ago, and I've been attending YFC rallies ever since."

"Oh, yeah? That's great!"

"And as a matter of fact, I've already asked to be the one who takes you around Ontario this coming week to your different meetings."

"Well, that's great, that's grand, padnah. We're going to get to talk about all this."

"Yeah . . . I guess we will. . . ."

And we did talk a great deal. I had been able to get a week off from my job, and as we traveled I told Redd what had happened in reform school and how I'd come to Frankford to live with the Adamses and to work at Bata Shoes.

I told him about seeing his film *Oiltown, U.S.A.* one night in Trenton, and we talked about my father. Redd wanted to know if I still hated him, and I told him that my feelings had changed. We talked about how God changes people, and both of us had stories that testified to that. Redd's press releases always mentioned the "full life" he led as a Hollywood movie star before being saved in May 1950. Redd hadn't been down the same road I had traveled, but he still knew all about wandering too far from God and feeling empty and lonely.

I heard his testimony many times that week as he spoke in different Christian Business Men's Committee breakfasts, luncheons, and banquets. He always sang, too, and he let me choose some of the songs. I especially liked to hear him do

"Christian Cowboy," "Beloved Enemy," and his best-known song, "Each Step of the Way." He'd get up and announce the song and say, "I've got my padnah, Paul, here. He's takin' me around this week in his 'doggymobile,' and I'm singin' this one for my padnah."

By the end of the week, Redd Harper and I had become best friends, and we would remain so for life. At the end of his tour, his last appearance was in a TV studio in Hamilton, Ontario. I stood behind the cameras, watching him tape the program, and as he closed by singing "Each Step of the Way," I remembered the first time I ever heard Redd sing that song—while I was projecting his film *Mr. Texas* in the rec hall at Bowmanville reformatory. I thanked God things were so much different now, and I promised him I would follow Jesus "each step of the way."

TWELVE

ONCE A THIEF, ALWAYS A THIEF?

I'm a gospel magician today because of Jimmy Lake, who performed at a YFC rally a few weeks after Redd Harper's tour was over. I watched in awe as Jimmy's long, skillful fingers did brilliant tricks with silks, coins, and other objects. He was known as a "master in silks," brilliantly colored handkerchiefs that he manipulated with a sleight of hand that had you baffled and delighted at the same time.

Afterward I went up and talked with him. I was a little confused because my experiences with the coven had convinced me that Christians just couldn't be involved in magic.

"I used to do card tricks, but no more," I ventured tentatively.

Jimmy smiled and said, "I don't do card tricks either." It turned out he had definite standards on what he did with illusions on stage and what he would not do. Jimmy Lake impressed me. He had formerly been President of the International Brotherhood of Magicians but was not doing magic as strictly entertainment any more. Since becoming a Christian, he had switched to using illusions as object lessons to teach spiritual truths.

Jimmy had been converted at People's Church in Toronto under the ministry of Oswald J. Smith. Before coming to Christ, he had done magic only part-time, but after thoroughly studying God's Word, he went into full-time ministry as a gospel magician.

"I get people's attention with the tricks," he explained, "and then I put across what I want them to know from Scripture. You go through the eye gate, and that opens the ear gate, and finally you get through the heart gate!"

I recognized the same terms John Bunyan had used in writing *Holy War,* which I had read after finishing *Pilgrim's Progress.* Jimmy Lake's approach to the "eye gate" got me thinking: *Maybe I could use my magic tricks again some day.* But I knew I wasn't ready yet. Our local YFC leaders wanted strictly pros to appear at their rallies—no amateurs, and I was still an amateur. Several years later, Jimmy would be instrumental in helping me become much more professional in doing illusions.

There are thousands of people, Christian and non-Christian, who are registered in magicians' brotherhoods across the world. Almost all of them perform part-time for little pay or for no pay at all. A lot of people are in it strictly to entertain, but the true gospel magician practices his craft with a heart of dedication. That night at the YFC rally, I saw that dedication in Jimmy Lake and decided I wanted to follow his example.

I spent the summer of 1959 much as I had during the previous two summers—touring for YFC or World Vision, speaking, and showing films throughout Ontario, Quebec, and the Maritimes. By the end of that summer, the call to full-time ministry was stronger than ever, and I knew I had to leave Bata Shoes and get more Bible training. Then I would be ready for whatever God had for me.

In September 1959 I moved to London, Ontario, to attend the London College of Bible and Missions. I also kept my work going with YFC, going out to speak when I was asked. Part of my YFC ministry was called "Life Line," which took me into jails and halfway houses to try to help young kids in trouble with the law. While visiting a Salvation Army halfway house in London, I met Tom, a young man of around sixteen who had already done one stretch in reform school for breaking and entering. As I shared my story with him, recognition seemed to dawn in his eyes. He asked me, "Did you say you grew up in Sarnia?"

"Yes, after I shot that woman, I came right through London as I ran from the police."

"And your last name is what?"

"Powers—my real name was LaVern, but I took the name Paul a couple of years ago."

"Don't you know me? I'm Tommy. I'm your stepbrother, the little kid you had to take care of."

"Tommy!—of course! How I hated all those dirty diapers!"

We talked for a long time after that, and I shared how God had touched my life and changed me. Before I left his cell, Tommy bowed his head and accepted Christ as his Savior.

I hadn't been in London long when I got a chance to go over to Sarnia—sixty miles west—as part of a crusade with Barry Moore. As soon as we arrived, I made a beeline for the old house on Cameron Street. When I knocked on the door, David opened it. The second he saw who it was, he slammed the door in my face.

I went around to the back of the house and knocked there. My father was just coming up from the basement, and he opened the door. There we were, face to face, for the first time in over seven years. The last time I had seen him he had said, "Send him to hell, for all I care!"

Dad hadn't changed much. He had that same dull look, and the whites of his eyes were still tinted with yellow from all of his drinking. He didn't smile. He didn't even looked surprised as we stared at each other for what seemed like more than a minute.

I tried to smile and said, "Hello, Dad."

My father's expression never changed, and his cold grey eyes bored through me. Finally he spoke: "What are you doing here?"

"I just want to talk to you for a few minutes. I want to apologize for sending those rude letters right after I became a Christian."

A trace of a wry smile twisted his lips, and he sort of shrugged. "I heard from Tommy—he wrote me about seeing you."

"Yes, Tommy and I had a great talk. I'm trying to help him with some Bible study."

Amazingly, my father became curious and wanted to talk. He offered me a beer, but I said, "No, thanks." I told him I wanted to be friends with Tommy and I hoped to come back and visit him again. "Maybe I can bring Tommy down sometime if I can get him out on a weekend pass from the halfway house," I offered.

Betty came into the kitchen and joined the conversation. I was expecting a lot of animosity, but perhaps having my father present held her in check. She wasn't warm, but she wasn't hostile either. She did enjoy picking at me, though, saying things like, "Now I suppose you think you're better than us, don't you?"

"No, Betty," I replied. "I'm one of the worst, but God loves me anyhow. That's all that counts."

Dad just sat there listening as he took another big swallow of beer. We talked some more, and eventually they invited me to stay for supper. Teachers and friends at Bible college had helped me understand it doesn't pay to aggravate people while trying to witness, so our conversation stayed pretty general. I got caught up on where everybody in the family was and what they were doing. And, of course, I told them what had been going on in my life.

As I left, I invited my dad and Betty to come hear Barry Moore at the YFC meeting that evening. They said they weren't interested. I tried to hide my disappointment, promising to try to come back and see them again and to bring Tommy with me, if possible.

I got back just before it was time for Barry to speak, and I told him about seeing my folks and even staying for dinner. Barry put his arm around my shoulder and said, "Now don't push it too hard, Buddy. Good opportunities here—just keep praying for them, and you do right by your brother Tommy."

Over the next year or so I visited Tommy frequently at the Salvation Army home, which was for kids from broken homes or bad environments—one step before reform school. He was never allowed to go with me over to Sarnia to see the family, but he was given permission to attend some YFC rallies in London. He seemed to enjoy the speakers a great deal. He also finished a correspondence course with Moody Bible Institute and eventually was released and went back to Sarnia to live with Dad and Betty.

I continued with a full schedule for the next two years, attending classes at London College of the Bible, speaking for YFC, showing films, and working with the YFC Life Line Department. In the summer of 1961, I spent several weeks taking classes relating to youth ministry at Moody Bible Institute in Chicago. While there I also got involved with the Pacific Garden Mission, which did a special version of my life story on its famed radio program, "Unshackled."

Despite all my Bible college studies, I never did earn a degree because I was always too busy running here and there. Then in

1962 a door seemed to open when the London area director of YFC resigned and I was invited to come on the staff full-time as interim director.

I agreed, but rather reluctantly. I was still attending classes at London College of the Bible and Missions, and I just didn't feel comfortable in the role of director. My self-esteem was still a long way from healthy, and I tried to hide my lack of confidence by buying expensive clothes and a better car. Soon I was in debt way past my ears, and the modest salary paid by YFC never reached from one week to the next.

It was then I discovered that, although I had changed my name to Paul, larcenous little LaVern was still very much alive. I began taking small advances on my paycheck by dipping into offering envelopes that would come into the office by mail. My plan was rather simple: I would take an envelope containing a letter and cash, remove the cash from the envelope, and put the envelope in a drawer, with a note inside on how much I had taken. This way I kept track of what I owed YFC, fully intending to pay it all back as soon as I could.

But my fast life-style, which included dressing sharp to look good up front, keeping my car running, and spending large amounts of my own money taking kids out to restaurants after rallies, only got me farther and farther behind.

I was bound to be caught, and, ironically, a girl I had formerly dated was the one who turned me in. Carol was the YFC office secretary, and she began to suspect something was wrong but didn't say anything to me. Instead, she told Bryan, the director of the YFC Bible Club and Bible Quiz operation. Recently, I had started dating Bryan's sister, Penny.

I didn't suspect anybody was on to me until one day I couldn't find some of the envelopes that I had been carefully concealing in my desk drawer. I wondered if Carol had found them, but I had no way of proving it and wasn't about to ask her. That weekend we had a big rally at Beal Tech High School in London, and afterward we were all headed out for our customary fellowship time at a local restaurant. As usual, I found myself with no cash in my pocket.

As we loaded everything into the trunk of my car, I spotted a separate envelope containing the proceeds from sales at a book table that YFC had operated that evening. No one noticed as I quickly removed twenty-five dollars in cash and then continued loading songbooks and other materials, including a zippered money bag containing the evening offering—well over three hundred dollars.

I went on to the restaurant and was treating some of the kids who had attended the rally, when Claude Card, a YFC board member, came in, walked over to our table, and asked to see me for a minute. We stepped outside and he said, "Paul, the board would like to talk to you—right now, at Dr. MacKenzie's office."

I didn't quite know what was going on, but I had a strong hunch the jig was up. When I walked in, all of them were there waiting—Carol and Bryan, and several members of the London YFC board, including Gordon Duke and "Buzz" Winslow, an older man who was sort of a father figure. Now I was really worried, wondering if I could talk my way out of this or if the ax would fall right on my neck.

Buzz Winslow served as spokesman and got right to the point: "We have to deal with some things in your life."

I knew I was nailed, but all I said was, "I don't understand, what do you mean? Is there something wrong with the way I've been doing my job?"

Buzz pulled out a sheet that showed the offering and book sales for that night and said, "Someone recorded the amount of book sale money taken in this evening, and twenty-five dollars is missing."

I looked over at Carol and saw a flicker of triumph in her eyes. She must have counted the money before we started loading the car! I had lifted the twenty-five dollars, and there was nothing to do but admit it.

"Yes—I have it."

"There was no note in the book money envelope, and you didn't clear it with anyone."

Trying to make an excuse, I said, "Well, I am the area director—the kids were waiting for me and ready to go. Besides, I planned to put it back later."

Ignoring my noble intentions, Buzz bored in harder: "Paul, apparently this has been done before."

"Who says so?" I bristled.

"Can you explain these?" Buzz brought out all the envelopes that I had been stashing in my drawer!

"According to the notes you've made in these envelopes, you've taken nearly five hundred dollars."

Now I was in real trouble! I began getting very upset, thinking that Carol had ratted on me because I had dumped her to start going with Penny.

After a long silence Buzz asked, "Well, did you do it?"

"Yes, I've been taking money, but I've been trying to replace it."

"You don't make much money, Paul. How could you ever hope to pay it all back?"

"What do you want me to do about this?" I asked somewhat defiantly.

"You're going to have to pay this back. We're going to have to talk about this and decide how it can be done." The other board members in the room nodded in agreement.

"Yeah, well, while you're talking, I'm getting out of here," I exploded. Turning on my heel, I dashed out, jumped into my car, and drove across town to the YFC office. Opening the trunk, I got out all the materials, plus the offering bag for that night and hurried up the stairs thinking, *There's just no hope . . . you're dead . . . you're finished . . . you can't hold it together . . . you've fallen on your face, and the only thing to do is get out of here.*

I was miserable and ashamed. What would Mom and Dad Adams think? What about Jim Blackwood and Barry Moore? They were holding meetings out west, but what would they say when they came back? And then there was my father—and Betty. They would surely laugh and make all kinds of I-told-you-so remarks.

I opened the safe, put in the zippered bag full of money, closed the safe door, and spun the dial. *Well, at least they can't nail me for taking any of this!*

I was coming back down the stairs when two of the YFC board came through the door.

"What are you doing here, Paul?" Claude Card asked.

"I've brought back the offering and all of the quiz material and other stuff. The money's in the safe, and the rest of it is at the top of the stairs."

"Paul, you've got to deal with this thing," pleaded Claude. "You have to pay back what you've taken."

"No, I don't . . . I'm getting out . . . I'm going someplace else—anywhere but here."

"But we want you to stay," Claude protested. "We want you to deal with this and work it out."

"I'm not going to stay anywhere! Get out of my way!"

I handed Claude the keys to my office, practically shoved him aside, and ran out to my car. I roared out of the parking lot and decided to head for Hamilton, about fifty miles east. Penny lived in Hamilton—maybe she would help me somehow.

Along the highway not too far from Hamilton was a big stone bridge. As my headlights picked it out of the darkness at 70 mph., I was feeling sleepy, depressed, and despondent. *There's no hope for you now. Once a thief, always a thief. You were stupid to think you could overcome your past! Your Christianity is a sham—you were kidding yourself. Deep down you're a thief and a killer, and you always will be!*

Then it struck me, *Why not drive right into the concrete abutment of the bridge? It will be all over in one grinding second. You'll put yourself out of your misery, and everyone will be glad.*

But I stayed on the road and went right on across the bridge. I knew I was afraid to die. I wanted to end it, but I was terrified because I wasn't ready to meet God. I knew Christ—I thought I knew God's love—but now it all seemed to have trickled away. Nothing was left but emptiness. Just outside Hamilton I decided not to bother seeing Penny. Her brother, Bryan, had undoubtedly called and told her all about me, and what could I say?

No hope; there's no hope now, I told myself as I turned my car toward Toronto and drove on through the night. I had failed—utterly and completely—and I had no idea of how a Christian is supposed to handle failure. Bible college had never offered any courses on dealing with failure; everything had stressed "victory in Jesus." But I had lost. The old life had won, and I felt totally alone.

THIRTEEN
"Uncle Paul, I Still Know Jesus!"

The pain shot through my chest like a bolt of electricity. Then it spread to my left arm and hand, leaving them practically paralyzed. I fell to the floor of the apartment alcove, calling faintly for help as I writhed in agony. My stepsister, Donna, finally found me and called an ambulance. It seemed to take forever for them to come, as the torment in my chest grew worse.

"Looks like a heart attack," said one ambulance attendant as they carried me out. I couldn't believe it! I was too young to have a heart attack—or was I? Maybe God was serving judgment on me after all I had done to hurt so many people. One attendant kept working on my chest as the other drove through heavy traffic to Toronto General Hospital. I prayed we'd get there soon. My chest felt like an elephant was standing on it, and my tongue was stuck to the back of my mouth.

My torture continued as I was rushed into emergency and hooked up to heart monitoring machines. Finally the crushing pressure subsided a little and somebody said, "It's going to be OK, it's not his heart . . . he had a stress stroke." Later I discovered that a stress stroke is like getting a charley horse in your heart muscle. The pain is incredible, and you are incapacitated for while, but there is no heart attack.

I stayed in the hospital several days and then went home to my stepsister's apartment. I had been living there ever since arriving in Toronto in disgrace after being caught "advancing my salary" at YFC. I still didn't like to call it stealing—I had always intended to pay back the money. Besides, my former girlfriend had set me up to get revenge.

I wasn't able to work for several weeks, and as I regained strength, I had a lot of dreams that riddled me with guilt. I had failed everyone who had trusted me—God, the people of YFC, Mom and Dad Adams, Barry Moore. I had turned out to be like the thief who rejected Jesus, not like the one who trusted in him.

Once a thief, always a thief . . . , my conscience whispered. I kept remembering what Jim Blackwood would often say whenever we discussed people who had dropped out of ministry: "When a Christian worker sins, God can't use him again. He's a cracked cup—set on a shelf." I knew I was through as far as ministry was concerned. There just wasn't any hope. I'd spend the rest of my life selling shoes . . . at least I could still do that.

After moving in with Donna and Ed in Toronto, I had immediately contacted the manager of a Bata store downtown. He knew my name and my good reputation in the shoe business. I didn't bother to tell him about other things that were part of my reputation—how I'd been fired from Bata in the past for stealing money, and how I'd been forced to resign from YFC for "borrowing" money against my salary.

What he doesn't know won't hurt him or me, I told myself. *I've done plenty of good work for Bata, and I can sell shoes like nobody else. As for YFC, I got a bum deal—I would have paid that money back if I had the chance. . . .*

Trying to put my problems behind me, I plunged into my work at the shoe store and put myself under tremendous pressure, trying to make extra-high sales quotas. I didn't go back to drinking, but I did start smoking again—my usual pack and a half a day. My impossible schedule, combined with all the guilt and depression I kept bottled up inside, worked on me until that stress attack hit me one evening, just as I arrived home from work and was taking off my coat in the front hallway.

When I was finally able to go back to work at Bata, I had to be on a reduced schedule. I still worked hard—probably as hard as any average salesman—but for me it was cutting back. Every time I found myself in a hurry and under a lot of stress, I just remembered that pain, and that would slow me down. I didn't ever want that kind of pain again.

A few months later I was walking through Eaton's, one of the largest department stores in Toronto, when a little voice called, "Uncle Paul, Uncle Paul, will you show me a trick?" I spun around, and here was little blonde-haired Sandra, a young girl I remembered baby-sitting while I had been a student at London College of the Bible and Missions. I hadn't done much baby-sitting in those days because I had been busy with studies and working for YFC, but occasionally I would agree to watch the children of YFC friends, and little Sandra had been one of them.

She was about three or four at the time and *toilet trained.* I was glad about that, because I could still remember all those dirty diapers that I changed while baby-sitting my younger brothers and sisters. I had done a few magic tricks for Sandra to amuse her before she went to bed—things with silk hankies and sponge balls. She had thought I was a "real magician."

Her mother was nearby having a purchase gift wrapped, and we all talked for a few minutes. As I left them, little Sandra said, "Uncle Paul, I loved your tricks . . . I still remember about Jesus . . . I still know Jesus!"

"That's wonderful, Sandy," I called out as she grabbed her mother's hand and they headed up an escalator. "Don't ever forget—he's always there to help you!"

As I walked out of Eaton's I realized, *You've got to do something . . . maybe there's something you could still do for the Lord even though you've really fouled up your life.*

I went back home and sat for a long time, thinking about what Sandra had said: "I still know Jesus!" I still knew Jesus, too, even though he couldn't think much of me. Suddenly I fell to my knees and prayed, asking God to forgive me—for stealing from YFC, for being afraid to stay and make it right, for leaving in a rage and almost trying to kill myself. Maybe—just maybe— Jesus could use me, even though my life was such a mess.

Meeting little Sandra and asking God for forgiveness was a turning point. Until then I had never really asked him to forgive me for everything that had happened back in London. I had felt remorse and regret, but I hadn't repented for what I had done. I'd stayed outside of God's love and grace, wandering around like a prodigal. But when a little girl shouted, "Uncle Paul . . . show me a trick," I finally heard his call and came back to him.

In the next three weeks, everything seemed to happen at once. First, I moved out of my stepsister's place and got an

apartment of my own. Then I began attending the Avenue Road
Alliance Church, pastored by A. W. Tozer, one of the giants of
the Christian faith who was coming to the end of a long and
distinguished career. I was feeling good . . . like maybe life
would go right for a change.

One day Jack, my manager at Bata Shoes, called me into the
office. They had planned to open another store, and I had been
asked to be the manager. As I sat down, I thought Jack was
going to tell me everything was set. Instead, he told me that
because I had to be bonded to be a manager, they had done
some checking and found out about my problems at YFC.

"Paul, you didn't tell me you got bumped from YFC for tappin'
the till. Are you tappin' the till here too?"

"No, of course I'm not. You know I'm going to church and I've
stopped drinking. I've even stopped smoking cigars."

"Well, I'm sorry, but we're going to have to let you go. I'd like
to keep you, but when the higher-ups find out, there's no way,
and I'll be in big trouble."

I left Jack's office knowing my days at Bata Shoes were
numbered. I wandered out into the streets of downtown Toronto
and decided to drop in at Evangelical Publishers Bookstore,
where I had been spending a lot of spare time browsing through
books and occasionally buying one to read. Despite all my
problems, my thirst for reading had continued, and the E. P.
Bookstore was a retreat that I used often.

I browsed among the books for awhile, but they didn't seem
to have anything on "what to do when you lose your job." I
struck up a conversation with one of the clerks and learned that
their film library rental manager was leaving. I'd always loved
films, ever since I was small, and showing films was one of the
few pluses I had received while serving time in Bowmanville.

I decided to apply for the film rental manager job. A. J. Stewart,
manager of E.P. Bookstore, interviewed me—and he knew
about the problems I had had while working for Youth for Christ.
"If you can get their approval and recommendation, I'll hire
you," he told me. "YFC is holding meetings for all of its area
directors at the Royal York Hotel just down the street. This
would be a good time to go down there and try to talk to someone."

Why not? I thought. *No time like the present.* I walked the
seven blocks down to the Royal York Hotel. I had to walk

because my car had been repossessed. I waited around in the lobby for over an hour before I saw someone I knew. Finally a group of YFC people came out of the elevator, including Wes Arrum, who had become director of YFC for all of Canada, and Fred Koop, director of Toronto YFC.

I got out of my chair, took a deep breath, and walked across the lobby to intercept them as they appeared to be hurrying out for lunch. All *I* was going to have for lunch was humble pie, but I decided there was no better way than to dig right in.

I stepped into their path, and there was a long awkward silence. Then Fred Koop said softly, "Hi, Paul, nice to see you. What's happening?" He pulled me aside, and we talked in low tones. I remember him saying, "Things will never be the same, but I have some great memories of working with you."

Wes Arrum tapped Fred on the arm, saying, "We've really got to get going . . . Paul, it's been quite awhile . . . we were just headed out for lunch, and we're on an awfully tight schedule."

I could tell he wasn't really interested in talking to me, but I kept going—I had to. "Well, I'll just take a minute . . . I need a favor. I'm losing my job, and A. J. Stewart of E. P. Bookstore says that he'll take me on on a trial basis as his film rental manager if I can get your recommendation and approval."

Wes Arrum exchanged a knowing look with Fred Koop and then said, "I don't know, Paul, you left quite a mess back in London. How can we know we can trust you?"

"I can see why you would be skeptical, but I have straightened things out with the Lord, and I want to pay back the money I owe YFC. Look, Wes, I really don't have much chance if you don't help me. I'm begging you to give me a break."

The group of men shuffled nervously. About all I hadn't done is fall on my knees right in front of them in the lobby of the Royal York Hotel! It was becoming an embarrassing scene for all of us. Wes continued to shake his head and mutter about "hearing this kind of story before." I began feeling the same hopeless feeling that had overwhelmed me the night I almost rammed my car into the bridge. Just then Fred Koop spoke up and said, "Wes, I think we should give Paul a chance. He says he's made things right with God, and I think we should believe him. Everybody makes mistakes—we all need forgiveness and another chance."

Reluctantly, Wes decided to follow Fred's lead. The other two men nodded their approval, and for the first time in months I felt real hope again. Maybe God was opening a door once more after all!

"I'll go along on one condition," Wes said, "that you arrange with EP to take so much out of your salary each week and send it to the London YFC office until what you owe is paid off. Also, I think you should write a letter of apology to the London YFC board of directors."

"I'll send a letter tomorrow! I really appreciate this, Wes, and I won't let any of you down this time."

And so it was arranged. Wes Arrum called A. J. Stewart the next day and later sent a letter of recommendation. I was hired by E. P. Bookstore the next week. Over the next few months, I paid back every cent that I owed the London YFC office, and I even gave additional money to help them cover other bills they owed EP.

My schedule at EP included having Wednesday afternoons off. And after learning that Jimmy Lake, the gospel magician I had met years earlier at a YFC rally, lived just a few blocks from my apartment, I would often go over to see him. What he had told me years before at the YFC rally still stuck in my brain, and I wanted to start practicing my illusions and tricks again. Practically every Wednesday afternoon I'd walk over to Jimmy's place, and he'd show me how to improve my techniques.

To get to and from Jimmy Lake's home, I had to go past the Toronto Zoo. There was usually a gang of kids—around eight to ten years old—kicking a soccer ball, and sometimes I'd stop to watch. One day they kicked it my way and I kicked it back. They did it again. Finally they became curious and came over to say hi. I started talking with them and then remembered that I had a couple of tricks in my pocket—a sponge ball and some small silks that I had used while practicing with Jimmy Lake. This was a good time to try my skills, so I said, "Want to see a trick?"

A gang of ten-year-olds always want to see a trick, and they all chorused, "Yeah! . . . sure . . . what kind?"

I took out the silks, and before their eyes the blue one became red, and the red became yellow.

"How do you *do* that?" they all wanted to know.

"Well, I have to be going now, but I have next Wednesday off. You be here about this time and I'll show you."

The following Wednesday the kids were there, and I showed

them more tricks. They were fascinated, and soon we became good friends. For several weeks I would drop by the zoo almost every Wednesday to perform for my ready and waiting audience. Later I met a youth director from the Free Methodist church down the street and introduced him to the children. He eventually got many of them into his boys' club at the church.

I didn't think much about my brief friendship with the kids at the zoo, but apparently God did. I know now that way back then he was planting seeds in my mind and heart—seeds that would blossom into the ministry where he really wanted me.

It was during this period that I got back into practicing magic illusions in earnest. I joined Jimmy Lake's Fellowship of Christian Magicians, as well as the International Brotherhood of Magicians and the Society of American Magicians. I attended meetings regularly, making contacts with some of the best Christian illusionists of the day. Besides Jimmy Lake, there was Sid Lorraine, Johnny Gordimaine, and Bruce Posgate who wrote many books and articles concerning his craft.

With men like these for tutors and coaches, I polished my routines under their sharp eye and helpful critiques. Most magicians can easily fool the average person, but when you're trying to do a trick before the sharp eyes of real experts, it's another story. They would quickly spot sloppy technique or poor timing and tell me, "Your move was slow when you were doing the silks . . . you weren't blending . . . the hidden silk was obvious . . . look out for the dangling threads. You were sloppy when you let the dove out of your sleeve . . . we could see it . . . it wasn't tucked in properly."

They also critiqued the verbal part of my presentation: "When you're talking to the audience, you're too stilted . . . you don't flow . . . you're not relaxed. When you're quoting Scripture, you sound like a little kid trying to get through a Bible verse. You've got to take time here because the message is more important than the trick. Stop showing off."

I listened to every word of criticism. They were kindly but firm, and what they wanted me to learn most of all was that I was not there to entertain as much as to present the gospel. I never forgot their teaching and advice.

As 1963 flowed into 1964, I was becoming more and more involved at the E. P. Bookstore. A. J. Stewart liked my work and began trusting me completely with all aspects of the business.

As for "advancing anything on my salary" or other stupid ideas, I had learned my lesson and put all that behind me. I also quit smoking—this time for good.

I was doing much better financially, managing my money carefully and living in an apartment provided by a Christian youth center, where I had gotten on part-time. The center director had known me from YFC days, and he occasionally had me speak and do other duties in exchange for my rent.

I was busy on a hot August afternoon at the store when in walked Jim Fishback, an old friend from YFC days in the London area. Jim was now attending seminary in Toronto. With him were his two sisters, Margaret and Ruby.

I remembered Jim's sisters vaguely because I had come to the Fishback farm once years before on an errand for YFC. As I shook Margie Fishback's hand I noted that she was tiny—well under five feet and probably weighing no more than ninety pounds. Obviously, the word for Margie Fishback was *petite.* Her soft chestnut hair fell around her shoulders, and she had a lovely, radiant smile. But her grey-blue eyes were her most striking feature. They could be affectionate, bright and twinkly, and then suddenly change to look sad and thoughtful.

She's about Mom Adams's size, I thought as I said, "So you're one of the younger sisters? Are you married?"

The question caught her by surprise, and she quickly responded, "No, are you?"

I grinned and whipped out a little booklet by J. Edwin Orr entitled *How to Have a Happy Marriage,* saying, "No, but I'm thinking about it."

Margie blushed and stammered, "Well . . . I'm not, and I don't have time anyway. We just came in for some VBS supplies, and we have to go."

"What's your hurry?" I protested. "Why don't we go downstairs to the restaurant and have a cup of coffee or a cool drink?"

A little reluctantly, she agreed to go along, and all of us went down the steps to the Honeydew Restaurant.

"What would you like to drink? Their specialty is honeydew."

Ruby gave me a puzzled look and asked, "Beg your pardon?"

Mischievously, I turned to Margie and inquired, "Honeydew?"

She gave me a startled look and responded, "Honeydew *what?*"

"That's their special drink: honey, orange juice, and milk, and some honeydew melon juice—that's why it's called the Honey-dew Restaurant."

"Well, I guess I can try a glass," Margie said coolly. I could tell she didn't like me too much, but I continued to act friendly. As we talked, I learned she was in Toronto picking up some summer school classes in connection with her work as a teacher. And the more we talked, the more I liked her and wanted to be with her. Margie reminded me of my years at YFC, the kids, the laughter. I was hungry for friendship and the things that used to be.

As we finished our glasses of honeydew, Margie mentioned they would all be going to the Canadian National Exhibition the following Saturday.

"I can get Saturday off," I said impulsively. "Mind if I come along?"

Margie looked a little flustered, not quite knowing how to respond, but Jim saved me. "Hey, that's a great idea—meet us at my apartment over on Spadina Street and we'll go from there."

The following Saturday I thumbed my way into town and started looking for the address Jim had given me. When I finally found the number, I was standing in front of a funeral parlor! It turned out that Jim lived in an apartment in the back and covered his rent by doing janitorial work for the mortuary.

By the time I found Jim's door, I was over twenty minutes late. "We thought you had set us up and weren't coming," Jim teased.

"Well, I got here in plenty of time, but I've been looking for this place for about half an hour," I told him. "You didn't tell me you lived in a funeral parlor!"

Jim burst out laughing as he pictured me coming up to the door of the funeral parlor and not knowing what to do. I started laughing, too, and it became a big joke.

But Margie didn't laugh much. I learned later that she really had thought that I had stood her up. I could tell she was a little ruffled, but I pretended not to notice. Off we went in a car Jim had borrowed from a friend. In addition to Jim, Margie, and myself, there was her sister, Ruby, and her younger brother, Harvey.

We got to the exhibition grounds just in time for the opening, and as Margie stepped off the curb at the entrance she walked into a puddle and tripped. I grabbed her arm to steady her, saying, "Watch it . . . you don't want to wind up in one of those slumber beds back in the funeral parlor, do you?"

She had to smile at that, but she didn't smile as we got to the turnstiles and the ticket taker charged me for one adult and one child's ticket. I told her, "You gave me the wrong change; I need two adults."

"Oh," the ticket taker said, a bit flustered. "I thought that was your daughter!"

Margie bristled a little but finally laughed. She'd been mistaken for a child before, and she was a good sport about it. For the rest of the day I teased her whenever we came to a puddle, saying, "You better not fall in there, you might drown."

Margie and I made our own twosome, walking along behind the others throughout the morning.

Neither of us liked the rides, so we went through the home shows, looked at different displays, and talked about being parents and how we would raise children—how we would discipline. The more we talked, the more comfortable I felt with Margie. As she relaxed, it turned out that she had a marvelous sense of humor. And it was also plain that we both really loved Jesus.

By lunchtime we decided to split off from the others, and so we made arrangements with Jim, Harvey, and Ruby to meet them later. We went over to the band shell to hear a concert and get something to eat. Just before lunch, I had stopped holding her arm when we came to any steps or puddles and we started holding hands. Although I didn't realize it, I guess I had fallen in love with her.

We spent the afternoon walking around, talking some more, learning that we both loved music and reading good books. She told me about her teaching work—how she had been a missionary teacher in Maniwaki, Quebec, with a class that included Indians as well as white children. Illness had forced her to return home, and she planned to begin teaching near Tillsonburg that fall.

As we walked through the Canadian National Exhibit, I marveled at how lucky I had been to find someone who was so much fun—along with being bright, creative, and with such spiritual depth. Margie made me feel like a person—like the person I had always wanted to be. Not the Paul Powers who had been madly dashing around directing YFC rallies a few years before, trying to be someone he was not.

It was of no advantage to Margie to be nice to me. I was a nobody, just a guy who rented films. But I had so much to gain from her friendship, and Jim's too. I had always liked Jim and admired his family, which had a love and warmth that I had never known.

As the day drew to an end, Margie invited me along to a supper engagement she and the rest of them had with a family who had been missionaries in China. "It would be fun to stay here," she said, "but we've promised to go and we have to keep our commitment."

Dinner turned out to be much more enjoyable than any of us thought it would be. We stayed and talked awhile, and then Jim offered to give me a lift back out to my apartment. Margie and I huddled in the corner of the backseat, talking. And just as we pulled up to my door I said, "Good night," and kissed her.

She gave me a surprised look but then said, "I really had a great time."

We had come a long way from the bristly cold drink at the Honeydew Restaurant a few days before.

"I'll write to you," I told her as I got out of the car.

As they drove away, Margie told Jim, "Paul won't write to me. He just had a nice day, but he won't write." She didn't think I was really serious and, to be honest, I didn't think I was really serious either—at least not that night. But we would both turn out to be very wrong about that.

FOURTEEN

"WILL OUR FOOTPRINTS WASH AWAY?"

"Then your parents say it's OK to go? And you'll play for the meetings? Margie, that's terrific! We'll have a special time, I promise you. We'll leave Friday—I'll pick you up!"

I hung up the phone feeling happier than I had in years. The last eight weeks had gone by so fast, and so much had happened since that day Margie had walked into the E. P. Bookstore. After saying good night following our Saturday at the National Exhibition, I found myself writing to Margie by Sunday afternoon! And I wrote a second time on Wednesday of that week. Then Jim Fishback phoned and said, "I'm going down to the farm at Tillsonburg for the weekend—want to go along?"

It happened that I was clear, with no speaking responsibilities all weekend. "Great," he said. "We'll leave early Saturday."

Jim hadn't said anything to Margie about my coming along, and I totally surprised her. She had gotten my letters and was literally headed for the mailbox to send me a reply when I showed up. Instead she just handed me the letter saying, "You might as well read this, but it's even better that you're here. It's so nice to see you again, Paul!"

We had a great weekend, and if we hadn't fallen completely in love the previous Saturday, we did over the next two days. On Saturday I cut their lawn—half an acre—and later I helped her father get rid of a hornet's nest under the eaves. That evening we played Monopoly and popped corn, and I got to know her parents better. Dad Fishback was kind of cautious at first, but later we would become solid friends.

On Sunday we attended their church, which turned out to be pastored by an old friend of mine from Bible college, Lambert Baptist. When I left to head back to Toronto on Sunday evening, I told Margie I would write some more, and I did—two or three times a week for the next several weeks. She wrote back, and when I could, I'd get away to the farm to see her.

Soon our letters started to include the phrase, "I love you," and I seemed to be walking about two feet off the ground. I had begun working with a Free Methodist youth group in Toronto that fall. And for the Canadian Thanksgiving weekend coming up in October, they had called and invited me to speak at a big weekend retreat at a camp north of Kingston, over a hundred miles east of Toronto. I knew how brilliant Margie was on the piano, and I called to see if she could come along and play for the meetings. I did it all very properly, asking her dad's permission first, and after a minute of silence, she had come back on the phone to say she could go.

We agreed to rendezvous at her sister's apartment right after she finished teaching school and I got off of work on Friday afternoon. Effie had just gotten married and was living in an apartment in Mississauga, a suburb just west of Toronto, right on Lake Ontario.

We both arrived at almost the same time, between four-thirty and five o'clock. I had a diamond ring with me, purchased at Eaton's just a few days before. My original plan called for asking Margie to marry me up at Echo Lake in some romantic spot at just the right moment. But as I walked into the apartment, I knew I couldn't wait any longer.

I went into the bedroom where Margie had been packing. I hugged her close and kissed her and said, "I want to talk to you."

"OK," she said, looking a little puzzled. She could tell I had something on my mind.

"Margie, we've talked about getting married . . . I really do love you and I know you love me." I took out the diamond and asked, "Can I put it on your finger?"

Margie's face was a study in contrasts. At first she had a look of sheer delight, but it quickly turned to almost sheer terror.

"Oh no, no, no!"

"Please, Margie, do you love me?"

"Oh yes, Paul, you know I do!"

I slid the ring on her finger—a size six that was way too big.

Then she started to cry, murmuring, "My parents don't know!"

With my arm around her, I was trying to console her and convince her at the same time. "Margie, it will all work out. Your dad likes me."

"Yes, but he didn't think you would want to marry me!"

Effie walked in and wanted to know, "What's wrong? What's going on?"

"Nothing," I said. "We're just glad to see each other." Later, when Margie told Effie about the ring, she was delighted, but she understood about Margie's concern. The Fishbacks were a traditional German family, and you didn't get engaged to a Fishback daughter until you asked her father for her hand.

So Margie put the ring back in its box and slipped it into her purse. We jumped into the car and headed for Kingston, almost two hours away. As we drove along, she took the ring out and put it back on her finger, but she kept her hand over it. It was as if she wanted to wear the ring, but she couldn't let the world know she had it—not yet.

Along the way we picked up two teenagers who were going to the camp and then went on to Kingston, arriving around seven. There was a little time to spare before meeting a couple of carloads of other people. We all planned to caravan north to Echo Lake, over twenty miles of twisting roads, as soon as everyone had some dinner.

Margie said she didn't feel like eating, and we decided to take a walk along the beach, which faces the Thousand Islands just a few miles off shore. It was perfect fall weather. The maple trees were a tapestry of red, yellow, and gold, and the sun danced on the water as it rolled in across the sand.

As we strolled along, arms around each other's waists, we talked—about everything. How would we approach her father? What would I say? How did we feel about a serious step like marriage? Could I support her doing youth ministry and managing a film rental business? Would I be a youth speaker or eventually become a pastor?

It was Canada's Thanksgiving weekend, October 1964, and I was a couple of weeks short of my twenty-eighth birthday. My goal was to manage my own film business, but I also wanted to be in ministry. I still had some debt—clothes, car deals, and other things I had bought on credit—but I had been paying it off. I owed a finance company, which hounded me like the

Mafia itself. But my debts didn't bother me that day. I knew Margie and I could make it together, but she still seemed a bit unsure.

I looked at my watch and saw that it was time to turn back. As we retraced our steps, Margie looked down and saw the footprints we had made coming from the other direction.

The wake from passing power boats had caused waves to wash in and wipe out some of our footprints. Margie said, "Maybe that's what will happen to us—maybe we'll be all washed up. Maybe our dreams are all going to wash away."

"No," I protested, "see our footprints just up ahead? They're still there. Where they got washed out is just the troubled waters we're going to face. Every marriage faces that."

"Yes, I know; but do we have it?"

I stopped, looked deep into Margie's eyes and said, "We've *got* to have it! If we love each other enough to fight for what we have, we'll make it. I think I've gone through enough to know what fighting is all about. What we have is worth fighting for!"

Margie was silent and thoughtful as we walked on farther. Then we came to a spot where there was only one set of footprints—mine. She had walked closer to the water with her sandals off, and her footprints had been washed away.

"What's your excuse for this one, preacher man?"

"Well, that's easy, that's when I carried you." She was wearing jeans, and I playfully swooped her up in my arms, saying, "See, you're so light!" As I held her high, she squealed and said, "I can't see you, I can't see you!"

"That's all right . . . I'm here, I'm here, and I'm holding you."

I put her down, we kissed, and we continued on, sometimes seeing two sets of footprints, sometimes only one. We got back to the hotel and sat in the restaurant, waiting for the others. Margie took out a Holiday Inn napkin and began to scribble.

I asked her what it was, and she said, "Oh, just a poem . . . about footprints in the sand." I didn't ask her any more then. Margie was always writing poetry, and I was constantly amazed at the beauty and depth of her work.

We drove on to Echo Lake. The next morning Margie played the piano during song time, and I preached a message called, "I Cannot Pray." Hundreds of kids from Free Methodist churches all over Ontario were there—teenagers from high schools along with college and career young people. I tried to explain what had happened when I worked for Youth for Christ and "borrowed" money without telling anyone. For awhile I just couldn't pray—God seemed distant, and I felt I was so unworthy because I had failed him. The young people listened intently as I went through the Lord's Prayer and explained how at that point I couldn't say, "Our Father . . . " I talked a lot about fathers and explained about my own father—how I had learned to love him after hating him and wanting to kill him for so many years.

That night my message was, "He Is There Though I May Fall." That afternoon, Margie had given me a finished copy of her poem, entitled "I Had a Dream." She told me about a dream she had the night before in which she was afraid her father would reject me when I asked to marry her. But writing this had given her the courage to go ahead with getting married, because God's promise to always be with us was the only possible way our marriage would work. As I read the poem, I understood what she was talking about:

> One night I dreamed a dream
> I was walking along the beach with my Lord
> Across the dark sky flashed scenes from my life
> For each scene I noticed two sets
> Of footprints in the sand
> One belonging to me
> And one to my Lord.
> When the last scene of my life shot before me
> I looked back at the footprints in the sand.
> There was only one set of footprints.
> I realized that this was at the lowest
> And saddest times of my life.
> This always bothered me
> And I questioned the Lord
> About my dilemma.
> "Lord, you told me that when I decided to follow You,
> You would walk and talk with me all the way.
> But I'm aware that during the most troublesome
> Times of my life there is only one set of footprints.
> I just don't understand why, when I needed You most,
> You leave me."
> He whispered, "My precious child,
> I love you and will never leave you.

Never, ever, during your trials and testings.
When you saw only one set of footprints
It was then that I carried you."

Following her poem, Margie added two Scripture references, Isaiah 63:9 and Hebrews 13:5. The Isaiah passage says, "In all their distress he too was distressed, and the angel of his presence saved them. In his love and mercy he redeemed them; he lifted them up and carried them all the days of old" (NIV).

And Hebrews 13:5 adds: "Keep your lives free from the love of money and be content with what you have, because God has said, 'Never will I leave you; never will I forsake you'" (NIV).

When I spoke that night I told about how Margie and I had walked along the beach, discussing our coming marriage. I told how I had held her up high, how she had laughed and protested, "I can't see you!"

And then I told my listeners, "But Margie knew I had a hold on her that would not let go. It's the same with all of us. We can't see Jesus Christ, but he guarantees in his Word that while we were yet sinners he died for us. That's his guarantee. You cannot see him, but he's there . . . believe that! There were many times when I seemed to be in utter darkness and I couldn't see him. I was flailing and lashing out, and sometimes I didn't think he could still love me, but always he was there, carrying me."

Then I read Margie's poem, and the kids sat spellbound. You could have heard the proverbial pin drop as many young people made life-changing decisions about trusting Christ.

The next day was Sunday, and at the morning service Margie introduced a new song that she had also written the day before.

It's a new life, oh, how He changed me
A new life, He rearranged me
A new life, richer and fuller
A wonderful, wonderful life.
It's a big life, oh, how He thrills me
A big life, oh, how it fills me
A big life, deeper and wider
It's a wonderful, wonderful life.
It's a great life, do not refuse it
A great life, don't ever lose it

> *A great life, why don't you choose it?*
> *A wonderful, wonderful life.*
> Chorus:
> *Gone is the old life and gone are its chains*
> *Gone are the wrinkles and gone are the strains*
> *Gone is the darkness and gone is the night*
> *I have found Jesus, the Truth and the Life.*

Everyone liked the new song, but as we chatted afterwards with some young people, there were mixed reactions to Margie's poem. Many of the kids liked it, but some didn't seem to understand it. Later she tried to have it published, but no one was interested. Nevertheless, the poem found its way into church bulletins and local newspapers. Eventually, it was used by churches all over Canada, then in the United States, and beyond.

You may have seen her poem—usually printed on a photograph of one set of footprints on a sandy beach. It has been sold in just about every form imaginable all over the world under the title "Footprints." But because she did not copyright the poem, Margie never got a single dime of royalty. It was always signed, "Anonymous" or "Author unknown."*

On Monday morning we packed, said a round of good-byes, and received congratulations from many young friends who had heard that Margie and I were planning to become engaged. They laughed a lot as we expressed our concern about how Margie's parents would feel when they heard our exciting news.

On the way back we stopped in Frankford for lunch, and I introduced Margie to Mom and Dad Adams. Margie and Mom Adams were both about the same height and could look each other eye to eye. They got along fabulously, and before we left they had a prayer with us about our new life together.

We laughed, sang, and joked all the rest of the way back to Tillsonburg, but during the last half hour of the trip our light mood became quietly serious. We were both silent for the last few miles as we anticipated how Margie's dad would feel.

Margie sat on her side of the car thinking, *Do we really know each other? I learned more about Paul's background this*

In recent years, we have negotiated with the Hallmark Greeting Card Company and C. M. Paula Publishing, who have both copyrighted the poem. Convinced of Margie's authorship, both houses have agreed to pay her royalties and sign her name to this world-famous piece of work.

weekend than I've ever known—we're so different—can it
work?

We got to the farm around 7:30 that evening and found
Margie's mother and father relaxing by a crackling fire. Margie
whispered something to her mother and then said, "Dad, I think
Paul wants to talk with you." Margie and her mother took off for
the bedroom, and I was left standing in the kitchen, staring
nervously at Mr. Fishback, a big rough-hewn German farmer
who was sitting there with his thumbs hooked in the bib of his
overalls, looking me up and down as if I were a steer he might
be considering for purchase.

He hadn't told me to sit down, so I stood. He said, "You want
to talk to me?"

"Yes sir."

"Well, did you have an accident?"

"No."

"Then what do you want to talk about?"

"Margie."

"What's wrong with Midge?" he said, using his pet name for
his daughter.

"Nothing's wrong with her."

"Then what are you talking about?"

"I think I'm supposed to say, 'I would like to have your daughter's hand in marriage.'"

There was a long silence as Mr. Fishback kept looking at me.
Finally he said, "What's wrong with the rest of her?"

I could see him grinning, and so I said, "All right, I would like
all of her."

Dad Fishback shoved his reading glasses back on his head
and said, "Do you love her?"

"Yes sir."

He looked a bit unsure. "Do you know what I'm talking
about?"

"I think I do," I answered.

"Boy . . . *you better know.*"

Taking a deep breath, I decided to say my piece: "Mr.
Fishback, I will love Margie and I will honor her. I will try to
make her life happy, but I'm not stupid. There are times when
she's going to be unhappy. And when she's hurt, I will be there
to comfort her. I don't want to take her away from your family,
but I want her to be my wife. I want to belong to your family!"

Mr. Fishback leaned back in his chair and looked at me for what seemed like at least a minute. Then he got to his feet, came over, and put his big calloused hands on my shoulders. The next thing I knew I was in a bone-crushing hug and he was saying, "C'm'ere, Son . . . let me welcome you to the family!"

FIFTEEN
A LOT OLDER THAN THEIR YEARS

"Paul, my keys are missing! I distinctly remember seeing them on the dresser when I was getting dressed for the wedding and putting them in my purse. Now they're gone and I can't get my luggage open!"

"OK, Mrs. Powers, let's have a look. Your husband has ways of making locks open up. . . ." I took Margie's suitcase and went out to the kitchenette of the small apartment we had rented near downtown Toronto. We had decided to spend our wedding night there before going on our honeymoon trip to the Echo Lake area above Kingston, a place with special memories of footprints in the sand and hopes for the future.

We had been married in Tillsonburg on Saturday evening, July 10, in the United Church. First Baptist, where Margie's family attended, wasn't large enough to hold the crowd of over one hundred, which included ministers and evangelists, as well as magicians and ventriloquists I had met through the Fellowship of Christian Magicians.

Mom and Dad Adams were there, and my father and Betty came, which told me he accepted me—at least a little bit. "There's nothing to drink," he had complained at the reception, and I had apologized saying, "Sorry, Dad. I guess we're just pretty straight-laced." Dad shrugged it off and seemed to enjoy himself anyway.

After the reception a couple of carloads of our friends tried to chase us, but we finally ditched them. After almost running out of gas, we got to our apartment in downtown Toronto at three o'clock on Sunday morning. We thought we had been pretty clever by bringing Margie's luggage, packed for her wedding trip, to the apartment several days before. That way her sisters or friends couldn't get into it and leave "interesting" little souvenirs. Now it looked like somebody—Margie suspects one of her sisters to this day—had the last laugh. There was *no way* she was going to bed without her nightgown, which was locked up inside the suitcase, along with all her other things.

"Oh, Paul, what are you doing? . . . You're going to ruin my suitcase!" wailed Margie as I started prying gently on the lock with a kitchen fork. I tried to get it turned, but it was stubborn, so I took the fork and bent one of the tines.

"Don't worry," I assured her. "I used to open locks a lot tougher than this . . . there! Got it! Works every time!"

Margie's eyes were wide with admiration. "Paul, I didn't know you could do that; you're wonderful."

"Oh, it's just a little sleight of hand I picked up somewhere," I said modestly. I hadn't yet told Margie much about our gang in Sarnia and how I had learned to open any ordinary lock by the time I was ten. Besides, it was kind of fun being a hero in my bride's eyes—why spoil it with true confessions?

The next morning we had a late breakfast and strolled along the street, enjoying the beautiful weather. The school where Margie would be teaching that fall was not far away, and she wanted to walk by and take a look at it. We had plenty of time to drive to our honeymoon cabin, and it was great having no pressure to be somewhere at a certain hour. As we strolled along, we heard music and thought it would be fun to drift over in that direction.

"Those are gospel songs," I said, and in a minute we came upon an open-air Campaigners meeting. I immediately recognized the leader—Mr. Wyman—whom I had met at People's Church.

"Paul! Great to see you!"

I introduced Margie and as we chatted, I noticed there was an accordion sitting there unused. The fellow who was supposed to play for the meeting hadn't arrived, and Margie picked it up.

"I'll play for you," she offered, and so for the next two hours we took part in Mr. Wyman's open air street meeting. Margie played a lot of the old standard hymns that street people would be familiar with—"Amazing Grace," "Abide with Me," and "The

Old Rugged Cross." Mr. Wyman did chalk talks, and then I did a few of my magic tricks and shared some of my testimony. Then Mr. Wyman preached a brief message, and several people made decisions for Christ.

It had been a great "first full day" of being married. Later, Margie and I would talk about how it had "made" our honeymoon. We left Monday morning and stopped in Frankford to see Mom and Dad Adams. They talked us into staying the night, and Margie and I slept in my old bedroom—the room where I had received Christ. We even took a walk up the hill behind the house for a close-up view of the telephone poles that had looked like crosses to me on the night that I had broken down and wept, feeling God's love envelop me.

On Tuesday we headed on over to Kingston and then turned north to a little village called Verona, just south of Echo Lake. I had begun attending the Free Methodist church in Toronto, and my pastor, Francis Caseman, had given us the use of his cabin on a little lake near Verona. After a bit of searching, we found it and, because of the hot July day and the inviting water only a few feet from the cabin, we decided to go swimming.

It looked as if we had the whole lake to ourselves, so we didn't bother with suits and just went skinny-dipping. We splashed around in the cool but comfortable water and had just gotten back to the cabin and were in the bedroom toweling off when we heard a voice: "Hello? Hello? May I come in?"

Margie fled to the bathroom while I quickly threw on a bathrobe and stepped into the living room. Standing there was an older man who had obviously let himself in! "Hello, my son is your pastor in Toronto, and he asked me to drop in and check to be sure everything was OK with the cabin. I was here yesterday, but no nobody was here—actually, I was expecting you on Sunday."

As I chatted with Mr. Caseman, Margie walked out of the bathroom, completely dressed. Introductions were followed by a long awkward pause. He looked at Margie, and then back at me standing there in a bathrobe and finally said, "I think I've interrupted something . . . I'd better go!"

We waited until his footsteps faded away before daring to look at each other. Then Margie ran, slipped the bolt on the door, and we both collapsed on the bed with embarrassed shrieks of laughter.

We had a great honeymoon week at the cabin, just hiking, chasing snakes, collecting cattails and stones—and talking. We went down to Kingston and retraced our "footsteps" walk, this time sharing the confidence that our step of commitment had given both of us.

Our honeymoon was a time of getting to know each other much better. In all the months we had dated, I had seldom been able to see Margie alone. We were usually at her folks' farmhouse with other people always around. Our honeymoon privacy was threatened only once more. Someone dropped by and told us that some of the kids in town who had heard me speak at Echo Lake the year before were going to come out and "chivaree" us some night just for fun. Margie and I kept waiting to hear their mock serenade, but they never showed up, probably because it rained hard on several nights that week.

Then it was back to Toronto and back to work. Margie began teaching in a school in the Yorkville district, a tough neighborhood on Toronto's west side. I continued managing film rentals for the E. P. Bookstore. I also continue going out on weekends to do my "Gospel Magic with a Message" presentations for youth groups.

Later that fall I was invited to speak for a week at a Free Methodist church in Timmins, a good-sized city over four hundred miles due north of Toronto. The flyers that were distributed were supposed to advertise a week of meetings for kids ages fifteen to twenty-one. I planned to fly up on late Thursday afternoon after work and start speaking on Friday, continuing until the following Thursday. But when I walked into the church on Friday night, I was shocked to see that it was full of kids—but two-thirds of them were *little kids,* well below teenage level. I found one of the flyers advertising my coming and discovered the problem: instead of inviting youth "15 to 21," a misprint told the world that the meetings were open to ages "5 to 12"!

A few teenagers came, but only because the pastor had announced from the pulpit that the flyer was wrong. I got through the first session but felt awkward because all of my material was designed for teenagers, not younger children.

Later that evening, very discouraged, I got on the phone and told Margie, "They fouled the whole thing up with the flyer. I've got mostly little kids here, and I don't want anything to do with this. I'm just not a children's speaker."

"You've got to stay, Paul," Margie urged. "If you leave now, you'll get a bad reputation and people will think they can't depend on you. You've just got to stay."

I argued with Margie, but in vain. She convinced me I had to go through with the week, and so I asked her to contact Jimmy Lake and buy some other tricks from him that would be more suitable for younger children. She agreed to see him the next day and send the tricks up on the next bus from Toronto.

As I hung up and prepared for bed, I shook my head and wondered what would happen. It wasn't that I didn't like young children; I often remembered my buddies at the zoo with fondness. But I was a youth speaker—that's what I had planned to do until maybe becoming a pastor later.

At London Bible College, and when I took some summer classes at Moody in Chicago, all the emphasis had been on training to be a pastor, a missionary, or the new specialty—associate youth pastor. With my background, it had seemed natural to choose the youth area because I could share firsthand what God had done for me.

Besides, nobody with any ability went into children's ministry—that was for little old ladies. When some occasional young guy said he wanted to do children's ministry, he got those raised-eyebrow looks, and everyone wondered if he was sort of "funny" or something. There was also the financial side: the ones who really starved were the children's workers. They were the worst paid, and the least prayed-for, group in ministry.

When I came in on Saturday evening for the second program, to my amazement, most of the little kids were back. I didn't understand because I thought all they would want is entertainment. I had spoken the night before about youth problems, dating, social problems, peer pressure—things they weren't involved in at all—or so I thought. Because the package from Margie hadn't arrived yet, I got through Saturday night as best I could, trying to rearrange my presentation so it would cover a wider age span. I did some simple coin tricks and wove part of LaVern's story into my message. I told it in third person, as if LaVern were somebody else.

On Sunday afternoon the bus arrived with the package of items Margie had purchased from Jimmy Lake. That evening the room was as packed with little kids as ever, and I used a "Bible Tear" trick that featured a large strip of paper with the word *Bible* printed on it in huge letters. Then I ripped the strip of paper to shreds before the children's eyes, while commenting that some people want to destroy the Bible. They say they don't believe in creation or any of the other so-called miracles of the Bible—all that is fairy tales. But then I emphasized to the crowd that God would not leave anything in his Book that was a lie.

I closed my little talk by saying, "You can't really get rid of the Bible. Ripping it up won't change the truth of God's Word. . . ." And at that moment, in my hands appeared an intact sheet of paper with the word *Bible*. I finished by quoting Jesus' words, "Heaven and earth shall pass away, but my words shall not pass away" (Matthew 24:35).

The kids really seemed to like the "Bible Tear," and on the next two nights my illusions featured rope tricks. These tricks focused on the ideas that only God can remove sins and that, in God's sight, all sins are the same size.

On Wednesday night my object lesson was built around a "phantom box," another trick Margie had purchased from Jimmy Lake and sent on the bus. As I showed the audience that the six-by-six-inch box was totally empty, I commented that we try to appear that we are all right, with nothing wrong in our lives. Then I reached inside the "empty" box and pulled out dirty hankies, soiled socks, and other objects that represented sin.

As I did a different trick each night, I continued to tell parts of LaVern's story without revealing his true identity. On the last night of the crusade, I used an elaborate trick called "Twentieth Century," which involves three large silk handkerchiefs and a change bag. Explaining that the bag represented the life of LaVern, the young hoodlum I had been talking about all week, I manipulated the silks to show how God cleanses sin from our lives when we believe that his Son has taken away our sins through his sacrifice on the cross.

To climax the object lesson, I told the children, "The reason I know God can do this is because I'm really LaVern—the thief and the murderer you've been hearing about all week! Jesus cleansed my heart of all its sin and hatred, and he can cleanse yours too."

That evening many young people and some children came forward during the invitation. Later, in the counseling room, I talked to a nine-year-old boy about Jesus, feeling unsure that he really knew what he was doing. But as I went through Scripture passages with him from Romans and the Gospel of John, I could tell that he *did* understand. He was well aware of what sin was and where lies came from—the father of lies, Satan himself.

I got suspicious, thinking he was from a Christian home and had been taught all this since the cradle, but it turned out he had never gone to church or Sunday school and was telling me only what he had picked up during my week of meetings. I prayed with him, gave him a Bible, and sent him on his way with an encouraging pat on the shoulder. Later that night, alone in my room, I pondered what had happened. These younger kids were understanding a lot more than I thought. I *was* being effective with them after all! Was God trying to tell me something? No, it must be my imagination. He had called me to reach teenagers—of that I was sure.

When I got home and told Margie what had happened, she admitted that she and two other Christian teachers, who worked with her in the Yorkville school, had been praying for me all week. Much to my surprise, Margie told me, "Paul, I know you could make a great children's worker."

"But Margie, God has called me to reach youth . . . all my training has been in that area. . . ."

"I know that, Paul, and you do a great job, but I'm just telling you that you have a certain sensitivity and touch for talking with younger kids. I think you should pray about what that means."

A few days later I had some time off, and Margie invited me over to observe her classroom. She taught a combination of sixth and seventh grade—eleven- and twelve-year-olds who were a rowdy, tough bunch. Yorkville was the Haight Ashbury of Toronto, the center of the drug culture in the city. Many of these kids were the children of hippies and drug users who had migrated to Canada from places like San Francisco. Many of them were from broken homes.

I did a few tricks for the kids and then chatted with them, not about religious things but just life in general. I asked them lots of questions—how they felt about cheating, lying, or stealing. Most of them responded by laughing and saying all that mattered was getting away with it.

When Margie and I were eating dinner that night in our apartment, I admitted, "Well, one thing is sure—these kids you're teaching certainly need the gospel—they're obviously a lot older than their years."

About that time Margie and I also got involved in the "Fish Net," a Christian coffeehouse for youth located in the Yorkville area. We'd go down at least three nights a week. I'd give my "Gospel Magic with a Message" presentation, and Margie would play the piano, counsel, and assist me for various illusions.

As we came and went, we would find smaller kids on the streets who were too young to get into the club. I found myself stopping to talk with them, and just like the kids at the zoo, they became my friends and told me their problems and troubles. I could see it in their eyes—a longing for love, for somebody who cared. Many of them were dirty and smelled bad, and it was obvious they didn't have much of a home life. I felt a strange hunger growing inside of me. I began realizing, *These young kids are more eager to hear the gospel than teenagers are!*

A few months later I experienced I guess what could be called the clincher when I was invited to speak in the Sunday school department of a Free Methodist church in downtown Toronto. After my presentation I gave an invitation, and a number of kids below age ten came forward. I spent the entire next hour—while the morning church service was in progress—talking with these kids, going over Scriptures and praying with them. I let them talk to me and tell me what was going on in their lives. Again I quickly saw that these kids could understand almost as much as adults could about sin. They knew about guilt—and they knew about loneliness.

I learned a great deal about loneliness that morning, about kids who were left with nothing more than a latch key. Some of them told me they would get so lonely they would start talking back to the television screen. Others, desperate to be with their friends so they could communicate, would hang around Coke parlors. They just couldn't bear going home, walking through the door, and finding themselves in isolation. Their moms and dads—if they were lucky enough to have both—wouldn't be home for hours, maybe not until late at night. I realized that in the past few months God had been putting me in touch with an entire generation that was desperately trying to find alternatives to isolation. That's why they used transistor radios, record players—whatever they could find to hear somebody else's voice.

It dawned on me then that the loneliness and isolation they described was exactly what I had experienced at the Guelph reformatory. The isolation these kids experienced was every bit as real as what I had felt when not even the guards would talk to me. Their parents wouldn't talk to them because they were too tired, or they'd come in well after their children had gone to bed. And so they were devising alternative families—kids their own age—gangs, if you please, because they had to have *somebody to talk to.*

As I talked with these kids, my own childhood flashed on my mental screen in vivid color. Between the ages of nine and twelve I had battled my own kind of isolation and misery. My real school had not been the formal building with teachers and desks and chalkboards, but that garage out behind Jimmy D's house. It was there I had learned about life—everything from drinking, drugs, and sex, to how to cross the wires on a car or break a window without making a sound. It was there I learned how to use a nail file to open locks, how to slip a coat hanger into a car window and have the door open in a few seconds, how to spot the cars that were easier to break into than the others.

True, most of these kids weren't even familiar with that kind of scene, but they and I had one big thing in common: a complete lack of the spiritual in our education and learning process. They knew little or nothing of God and even less about his Son, Jesus Christ. And they were headed down that same lonely road that I had traveled . . . almost to disaster.

After that morning in the Free Methodist Sunday school, I started getting more requests from churches in the greater Toronto area, and I found myself doing more and more things with younger children. And I didn't mind! Margie and I talked about it, and I finally admitted, "You know, maybe you're right . . . maybe God wants me to work with children even though it isn't the 'in' thing with ministry these days."

Margie threw her arms around my neck and just bubbled with joy. "Oh Paul, what do we care about what's 'in'? What you want to do is what God wants, and I've always known you could communicate with younger children."

Margie and I became a team, doing Sunday school and weekend meetings for children. We would both get off work and then drive anywhere within an hour and a half away to do a program. I developed a lot of presentations for younger kids, working hard to mix my tricks and illusions with stories that made a point. With my job at EP, I also had my pick of films that would appeal to children.

I also continued weaving LaVern's story into my presentations, but always in the third person, just as I had done in Timmins. At the end of the week, I would ask the children, "Would you like to meet LaVern?" A lot of them would actually get scared, but I quickly alleviated their fears by saying, "I'm LaVern, and I'm here to tell you that God can change anybody's life."

With her ability in music, Margie added a tremendous touch by doing all kinds of children's songs. We quickly learned that we couldn't always use the songs familiar to kids who had grown up in church. To try the familiar hymns and choruses like, "Jesus Loves Me," and "Turn It Over to Jesus," would only draw blank stares from many kids because they had never heard anything like that. So Margie wrote her own songs with a lower-key message that still got the point across. We still have to do that today.

By April 1966 I was ready to leave E. P. Bookstore and step out on my own in the film rental business. I bought a Gospel Films franchise and became the new Toronto representative, not only of Gospel Films, but of most of the other major studios producing Christian films at that time.

One evening as Margie and I were discussing our good fortune and the potential in our new film rental business, Redd Harper telephoned. It was good to hear his warm drawl. We chatted about a few things and then he said, "Padnah, what do you think about flying out here and teaming up with me for another crusade? I've got a lot of places lined up, all in the Los Angeles area, and I could use your help."

"Will it be like the one we did together in 1963?" I asked, remembering how I'd flown to California back when I was working with YFC.

"Similar, padnah, similar, only longer. This time we'll be out for two weeks at least."

Margie thought it was a great opportunity for me, and so I left her in Toronto while I flew to California to join Redd for two great weeks, holding meetings throughout the Los Angeles area. I also got to visit the famous Magic Castle in Hollywood, the home of top flight magicians who performed nightly for people who liked combining a fine meal with watching great magic acts. I got into the Magic Castle through the invitation of a magician who went by his stage name, "Senator" Crandall. I had met him in Toronto when he had been there to lecture at a magicians' meeting.

I flew back with a gift from Redd—part of the offering money he had collected—in my pocket, along with all kinds of hopes and ideas in my head. Before I left, my friend Senator Crandall suggested that I might want to be part of the Magic Castle someday. The thought of performing with some of the best magicians in the business was exciting. I also enjoyed the whole Los Angeles scene—the freeways, the fast-paced life-style. And obviously there were opportunities to reach thousands of people for Christ.

Already a plan was beginning to form in my mind: we could keep our film rentals and ministry to churches going in Canada and fly to the United States now and then to do things with Redd. He had already invited me back to help him with another crusade the following September, and he had urged me to bring Margie. Life was full, and we seemed to be in the fast lane, headed for success. What I didn't realize was that we would soon begin a wide detour that would take us to the brink of ruining not only our ministry, but our marriage.

SIXTEEN
TO DISNEYLAND— AND BEYOND

"You go if you have to, Paul, but you know what I think of the Hollywood scene. We've talked about it a hundred times, and you promised to quit all that."

"Margie, I don't have any choice. I signed contracts for these appearances months ago, and if I don't show I can be sued. We can even lose the house. Besides, we need the money."

"All right! You go, but I'm staying here. The traveling is getting to be too much, especially with Paula being so little. I'm telling you, Paul, we've wandered way off the path we agreed to take when we got married!"

I didn't really agree that we had wandered much at all, but I had no time to argue. As I hurriedly finished packing, the taxi rolled up. I kissed Margie and the girls and was gone. I can still see Tina and Paula, their little noses pressed against the frosty windowpane, with Margie standing behind them, unsmiling and worried.

It was a miserable way to leave on a trip, but there was little I could do. Margie would cool off, and when I got back we would talk. I'd help her see how far we had come and how God had blessed us during the past six years. It was January 1971, and overall life had been good to us. True, things had gotten a little tight in our film business, but we lived in a beautiful home in Don Mills, one of the nicer neighborhoods in the northern part of Toronto. We had a swimming pool, a couple of late model cars, and credit cards that we used often.

As the taxi sped down the parkway toward the airport, I thought about how all this had come about. After I'd gone alone to Los Angeles to spend two weeks helping Redd Harper with a crusade in 1966, he had said, "Padnah, the Lord really blessed . . . Why don't you come back in September to do some more meetin's with me? . . . And be sure to bring your little missus. Laura and I want to meet her."

"Pencil us in," I told Redd. "I'll check with Margie, but I'm almost positive we can come." And we had come, spending an exciting weekend with Redd and Laura in their beautiful home in Hollywood. We ministered with Redd on Friday, Saturday, and Sunday nights at a big church in Long Beach.

On the last night, after the final prayer and benediction, a man who looked very familiar came up to us and introduced himself. "Hello, I'm Walt Disney. I enjoyed your presentation and am wondering if you'd be interested in doing something for us at Disneyland or Disneyworld."

"Well, thank you, Mr. Disney, but I don't know if I'm good enough."

"You aren't the world's greatest magician," Disney admitted candidly, "but you sure know how to communicate with kids. How long are you going to be in town?"

"We fly out to Toronto tomorrow afternoon," I told him.

"Come down to the office in the morning and fill out an application," he urged. "I think we could use you."

The next morning we were at the Disneyland offices in Anaheim to fill out an application, and I also talked briefly on the phone with Mr. Disney. Then we caught the plane and flew back to Toronto so Margie could get back to teaching school and I could concentrate on getting our new film business going. The holidays were coming up—the best part of the year as far as film rentals were concerned.

I'd almost forgotten about Walt Disney's offer, but about a month later we got a phone call. Could I come down and do a couple of trial shows at Disneyworld in Orlando, Florida, in a week or so? *Could I?* You bet I could! I went down alone on that trip, did well, and soon I was getting more invitations to perform at both Disney parks, in Florida and California.

My appearances at Disneyland and Disneyworld got me other invitations—to Six Flags Magic Mountain in Atlanta, Busch Gardens in Florida, and then Knott's Berry Farm, the Japanese

Gardens, and the Crocodile Farm, all in the Los Angeles area. Whenever I was in LA, I'd try to drop by the Magic Castle, and eventually Senator Crandall, my friend and fellow member of the International Fellowship of Magicians, convinced me I should apply for membership there. I was accepted in 1968 and invited to perform on a few different occasions, which I consider a highlight of my magician's career.

Soon our lives took on a distinct and hectic pattern: during the summer Margie had vacation time from teaching, and the film business was slow. That's when we would concentrate on ministry in churches, camps, and daily vacation Bible schools in and around Toronto. Later we branched out to include much of Ontario, also getting into Quebec and New York State.

Following our summer ministry work, we would gear up for the big holiday rush on film rentals, which would last until just after Watch Night services on New Year's Eve. Then we would hop on a plane and head for the States—to LA, Florida, or Atlanta—to perform in mostly secular settings. Occasionally I would do something with Redd Harper in Los Angeles, but for the most part I was entertaining children in some of the biggest amusement parks in the U.S.

This routine had to take its toll, and one of the first things that was affected was Margie's teaching career. Early in 1967 she went with me on a trip to the West Coast, and when we returned she told me she simply could not hold down a full-time teaching position and be gone so often from classes. She decided to resign from full-time teaching and later did substitute teaching, particularly in the fall and late spring, reserving the winter months—January through March—to travel with me.

Our "winter vacations" to the States were enjoyable for several reasons: it was a thrill to be invited to perform at top amusement parks, the pay was excellent, and the weather was a lot warmer than Toronto's. About April we would usually migrate back up to Toronto and concentrate on the film rental business, which was strong around Easter. Then we would move into the spring and start gearing up for our summer ministry.

During the first few years, Margie enjoyed going on the trips and seemed comfortable with our fast-paced routine. She traveled with me throughout the winter and spring of 1968, right up to the time she had Tina, who was born in May. She didn't take part in summer ministries that year, but she did join me the following summer. Bringing Tina along, we ministered together in Canada, Pennsylvania, and New York State.

Paula was born in January 1971, but by then our lives had started to unravel just a bit. Never a genius at handling money, I soon found myself getting deeper in debt with the film business. We just weren't minding the store at home enough, but I was enjoying all of the traveling and entertaining big crowds in famous places too much to notice. We would leave our film rental business in the hands of three college students I'd met at church or through YFC contacts. They kept things going but would let bills go unopened for weeks at a time while we were gone. In addition, one of them was quietly tapping the till.

Soon we were overextended on buying films for rent, not having enough money to pay for them. When my agent finally sent a check for an appearance I would make in the States, I would try to pay a bill here and there, but more than likely I would say to Margie, "We've been under a lot of pressure . . . let's take the kids and fly over to New York for a few days. There's a magician performing there that we should see, and you can do some shopping too."

And so, whipping out our ever-ready credit card, we'd hop on a plane and soon be in New York or Chicago—or any place away from pressure and responsibility—spending money we didn't have on good times and toys. My taste in toys ran to tricks and illusions that I could use in my shows, and the price tag was usually high. I soon had a garage full of paraphernalia that had cost thousands of dollars, most of which I had used only once or twice, if at all.

By 1972 reality should have told me that we were just one step from bankruptcy. Instead, my taste for fantasy and the fast, exciting life kept me blinded to our real situation. The truth was, I had drifted spiritually—doing less and less ministry in churches and Christian camps and more and more entertaining in secular amusement parks.

I had become cynical about Christian ministry, often observing that churches were cheap and not very responsible about paying on time. Disneyland, Knott's Berry Farm, and places like that paid well—and quickly. As I faced choosing between taking a program at a church for thirty dollars or performing at a secular amusement park for three hundred dollars, it was all too easy to go where the money was.

As early as 1970, Margie had started to see where we were headed. She talked to me about the changes she saw in me and our ministry together. I brushed it off at first, but eventually I had to admit that I was feeling increasingly bitter about the way churches treated outside speakers such as ourselves.

We came through the fall and holiday season of 1971, and I had agreed to stop doing secular performances. But I found myself with several signed contracts that I could not break, and that's when I headed for the Coast alone on that January morning.

For the next few months I alternated between doing secular appearances in California, Florida, and Georgia, and flying home when I could. The tension between Margie and me did not diminish. In fact, it only increased as she pointed out that all of my commuting was using up a great deal of the money I was supposed to be using to get out of debt. Meanwhile she had been picking up substitute teaching jobs as best she could to supplement our income.

One night I flew in from Florida, but Margie wasn't in her usual spot outside baggage claim. Instead she had sent her brother Jim to meet me. "Margie was just too tired to fight the traffic," he explained. "She asked me to come instead." That didn't help relieve the tension at all. I heard a subtle message telling me that my wife and I were slipping farther and farther apart.

In April I had a full schedule in southern California, including Knott's Berry Farm, Disneyland, the opening of a huge new supermarket, and several supper clubs. Margie had stayed in Toronto, but I called and pled with her to meet me in Los Angeles during her spring break from substitute teaching. Reluctantly she agreed to come and bring the children.

By then I had made some good money doing the secular appearances, and, despite all the commuting back and forth, I still had a few dollars in my pocket. I was convinced that I had to keep going with the secular work to get completely out of debt—even into the summer months which were normally devoted to Christian ministry. I decided I would talk to Margie about this when she arrived on the Coast.

When I met Margie and the girls at the plane, she told me that the Easter film rental business had not done well. She felt the college students who were managing film rentals for us needed more supervision if we were going to save our failing business.

It appeared that churches were tired of ordering films to cover holiday programming. We had seen this trend during the Christmas of 1971, and it was continuing.

When Margie gave me the news that the film business was continuing to slide, I became even more convinced that I had to spend at least part of the summer doing secular work in amusement parks in the U.S. when the tourist season would be booming. But I didn't mention it right away. *Let her settle in, and then I'll bring it up,* I told myself.

A couple of days later we left Tina and Paula with the Harpers and headed down toward Whittier to have dinner with Virgil and Eleanor Wemmer, good friends who had a thriving film rental business going in that area. It was a Friday night, we were in slow freeway traffic, and I decided that now was as good a time as any to tell Margie I would have to do more secular work during the coming summer. But when I started to explain, Margie began to cry.

"I can't take this anymore, Paul," she said with desperation in her voice. "We're in debt because we spend too much money. We're out here right now when we shouldn't be. We use credit cards without thinking, and we run up bills on things that we don't really need."

"But Margie, I've finally gotten a few engagements and some checks. Things are looking better, and if I can keep working the amusement parks this summer, I can really take care of most of our debts."

"Paul, you know that isn't true. You may be making some money, but you're spending it hand over fist on plane fares. Every time you get a few dollars in your pocket, you think everything's rosy. But it isn't."

"Margie, when we got married I promised I'd look after you. I'm doing my best to try to keep things together, and I don't understand what you're saying."

"Paul, you've always looked after us, but now we're in trouble. We're just living too well—in a nice house with a pool, traveling all over the country, spending money in hotels. But the worst part of it is that you seldom talk about Jesus anymore. And when you do present a program for a church, you're mechanical—I can tell your heart isn't in it. I'd rather be poor and go back to the old apartment than do what we're doing now!"

"How can you say that? We've had a lot of good times during

the last few years. We've traveled, we've seen things, we know a lot of people. So the film business has gone a little sour, we'll figure out a way to pull out of it. . . ."

"Paul, you're deceiving yourself. Can't you see that we're falling farther and farther behind? You take the checks you get from the amusement parks to cover the losses from the film library. And when you do get any money in on the film library, you use it to cover your travel expenses for running around the country. And then, to top it all off, you spend all kinds of money on magic equipment. We've got a garage full of stuff that you hardly use, just because you wanted to have something for one special show, or to impress one special person in the business."

"Well, I need those things—that's my business; I'm an illusionist. Today you've got to have better and better illusions if you want to make it."

"But Paul, we're *not making it!* You spend thousands of dollars on a piece of equipment, and it sits in the garage after you use it two or three times. Those things are toys to you, not tools that you use over and over. I'm telling you, we don't need this. We're not happy . . . the kids aren't happy."

"What do you mean, 'the kids aren't happy'? They love traveling and watching me perform."

"Yes, Paul, they watch you perform, but they wonder when you're going to stop long enough to read them Bible stories and pray with them again. You use excuses and say you're too busy. The truth is, you aren't interested anymore."

The conversation hadn't gone at all as I had hoped it would. Instead of being understanding, Margie was belittling and criticizing me. I decided to pull out my "ace in the hole" and tell her about a new illusion I could buy that could help me get all kinds of new engagements. "The Crazy Lady" consists of a phone booth into which an assistant steps. The door is closed, and then two giant razor-sharp blades are inserted into the booth, one at shoulder height and one just below her hips. The blades are shoved through the booth, giving the illusion that the woman has been cut into three pieces. For the final touch, the middle section is lifted out onto a nearby table, giving the additional illusion that her torso has been completely separated from her head and legs.

"It costs only three thousands dollars, Margie, and it's just what I need, not only for appearances in the amusement parks, but I can use it in churches when speaking to kids. And I can book the bigger churches and camps that will pay a decent fee. Then we can forget working for nickels and dimes at the smaller places."

"Three thousand dollars! Paul, how can we possibly juggle the money to pay for this?"

"Margie, with this trick, I can get all the bookings we need."

"And how do you possibly ship this back home? It must weigh over five hundred pounds. And how do we pay for it until you 'get all the bookings we need'?"

"Margie, it will all work out. I've got it all planned. I'll ship it up to Buffalo on the train and then come across the border and take it into to Canada piece by piece in the trunk. That way I won't have to make a claim on it at customs, and we won't have to pay any duty."

"Paul, is this a Christian way to look at this? And besides, how can you teach kids in church anything spiritual with this kind of thing?"

"Oh, I've got all kinds of ideas. You can illustrate the split personality, how there's a void in a life when there is head knowledge but no heart knowledge. . . ."

"Paul, do you realize what you've just said? You're talking about having head knowledge but no heart knowledge, and you want to cheat customs! Paul, you're living in a fantasy world. You've got to come back to reality! We're not trusting God anymore. You're just trusting people who can pay you the most."

"Margie, there you go . . . using spiritual platitudes to cut me down. You're just not being fair. You say I'm not trusting God, and yet you're the one who's always griping about money. You say we never have enough. Here I am, trying to figure out how to make enough money to pay our bills, and you put me down. As for spending all this money going back and forth, you know I've wanted to move down here to the States for a long time and just forget what we've been doing in Canada because there isn't enough money in it. But you want to stay near your folks, so I'm stuck with the traveling. Margie, we just can't have everything."

"Paul, we don't need everything. What we need to do is get back to where we were when we were first married!"

"You know we can't go back to that. We're beyond all that now. We have two children, a home, a business . . ."

"Well, maybe you can't, but I can. I was raised in a little country church and . . ."

"Oh, here we go again, the 'little country church routine'!"

"Well, I'd rather raise my daughters in a little country church where they can hear the gospel than in a house where their father says he loves Jesus but acts as if he belongs to Satan's family! Paul, I've had it! If you don't change, I'm leaving you and taking the girls with me!"

SEVENTEEN
BACK TO
THE PROMISED LAND—
AND POVERTY

Margie's words stunned me: ". . . I'm leaving you and taking the girls with me!" Our verbal battle, waged while trying to get through Friday night traffic on L.A. freeways, faded into silence. For the first time in our marriage, I was afraid—really afraid. I had never had much, and I could lose most of what I had accumulated, but my tottering self-esteem could never stand losing my wife and children. They were all I really had.

"We'll talk about it later," I said quietly, as we pulled into the parking lot of the restaurant where we were to meet our friends. "Let's try to have a nice time with Eleanor and Virgil—if we can."

Margie dabbed at her eyes, did some fast repair work with her compact, and we stepped into the Fireside Restaurant to meet our friends, the Wemmers, trying to act as if nothing was wrong. I doubt that we succeeded. I'm sure that Virgil and Eleanor could tell that we weren't happy. And instead of staying to talk as we usually did, we left early, using the excuse that we were both tired after a long week.

Coming back from Whittier, Margie sat silently in the darkness until I said, "Look, I've been thinking about it in the restaurant. I've got to admit that it doesn't look good, especially in California. With Walt Disney dead, things just haven't been the same at Disneyland. There's always a lot of hassle when I perform there. And in places like Knott's, I'm getting a lot of single night appearances but no long weekends. I think we need to pray about what to do."

"I have been praying, Paul," Margie said softly. "I've been praying that we can get out of this Hollywood kind of life. We've got a wonderful family and a great ministry, and I think all of that should come first. Then we just trust the Lord for the money."

I was silent for a long time and then said, "You know, you're right. We've got a lot of things to praise God for. It's been a good marriage, and I don't see why we would want to blow it up. I don't want to lose my kids. . . ."

"Well, you don't want to lose me either, do you?" Margie asked anxiously.

"No, I don't want to lose you, but I don't want us fighting. We just can't have that."

"Well, maybe we're both just worn out," Margie suggested. "Paul, I've been feeling so desperate—that's why I had to blow off some steam!"

"I know . . . I know. It's been hard for all of us. I think we should go home to Don Mills and try to really figure this out. It looks to me as if we've got to sell the film business."

"Paul, that's really not what I meant."

"I'm not sure if we can get our finances under control any other way, Margie. There's a fellow in Buffalo who has been wanting to buy us out for a long time. Maybe we should consider it."

We got back to the Harper's fairly early but chose to go straight upstairs to the apartment that Redd always let us use when we came to California. Tina and Paula were asleep, and soon we were too. I was tired—very tired. But I had already made up my mind. For more reasons than one, we couldn't afford "The Crazy Lady."

The next day I made a phone call and told the owner of "The Crazy Lady" illusion I was no longer interested. Later, as Margie and I had coffee on the Harper's patio, I told her I had made the phone call.

I reached across the table, grasped Margie by both hands, and explained, "I've got to have the family *together.*" Both of us wept as we hugged each other, but they were good tears, the kind that wash away bitterness and open the way back to being one again.

I also talked to Redd and asked him to pray for us as we decided what to do with our lives. Good friend that he was, he didn't say anything critical, although I'm sure he had seen plenty of signs of trouble. When we boarded the plane the next day, he hugged me, saying, "Padnah, I'll be praying for you and Margie. I know God will help you make the right decisions. Keep in touch."

When we got back to Toronto, we plunged into our summer ministry work, all the while trying to cope with the huge pile of bills. I turned all the finances over to Margie. "This really isn't my area—we both know that. You take care of it, and I'll help any way I can."

We decided to hang on to the film business—for the time being. Chuck Peterman, vice president of Gospel Films, called me a couple of times during the summer to talk about how things were going. Because he knew how every Gospel Films franchise was going, he didn't have to ask. He knew we were in trouble and that we owed Gospel Films a considerable amount for films we had purchased. Gently but firmly, Chuck began to encourage me to sell the business, but I held him off saying I wanted to see how things would go in the fall before making a final decision.

The summer went by quickly, and Margie was happier because we were home and doing what we were supposed to be doing: trusting God and ministering. Nonetheless, it got tougher each week as money grew short. Early in the summer we did some programs in American churches near Buffalo, and they had paid us promptly. Those checks, plus a few dollars that had been left in the bank, kept us going. But as we went into the fall, Margie struggled to find cash to pay even the basic bills. I began selling off magic equipment to other magicians, trying to raise a few dollars any way I could to keep our house payment current. Eventually I had to sell our newer car, leaving us with an old AMC Pacer for transportation.

As we headed into the holiday season, I kept hoping that some of the churches where I had recently done programs in the Toronto area would send checks. But as the days went by, no checks arrived.

To add to our troubles, the upswing we had expected in film rentals during the holidays did not materialize. The down trend that we had seen during the prior Christmas season and into Easter continued. Churches just weren't using as many films for special holiday programming as they used to.

By December we were down to rock bottom. With barely
enough money to buy food, we often wound up eating the
pabulum that we would usually feed Tina and Paula for breakfast. Pabulum for dinner just doesn't cut it, and Margie and I
began to bicker once again. As I sat complaining one cold day
just before Christmas, she urged me to go out and try to collect
some of the money churches owed us. I did so, only to spend
the most humiliating day of my life, being given "handouts" that
totaled not quite forty dollars. I got no checks in full payment
for programs that I had done.

It is no wonder that, when I came home on that night of
December 23, I was on the edge of some kind of breakdown. We
had rejected the "garlics and leeks of Egypt" (Hollywood) and
had returned to our Promised Land, but instead of finding milk
and honey, we had come upon poverty. What was God thinking
anyway?

Perhaps he was thinking that he had to bring Paul Powers all
the way to his knees before he could start putting things back
together again. The Golden Box incident and my brutal slapping
of Tina for "wasting a whole dollar" accomplished that. When I
struck her that night I was engulfed in guilt. I had never been a
perfect father—in fact, when the girls were small their crying
and dirty diapers put me on edge, reminding me of days long
ago when I had been forced to care for tiny children in the worst
kind of squalor and hopelessness.

Before getting married, Margie and I had agreed on how to
discipline any children God might give us. We would spank, but
only when it was absolutely necessary—and only to discipline,
never to beat or punish. Up until that night, I suppose I had
swatted Tina less than half a dozen times; usually it was a slap
on the wrist to keep her from touching something that would
break or that would harm her. But when I jerked her off the floor
and violently slapped her face, I was a different person. Or was I
really the same person that I had always been? Was LaVern still
crouching inside ready to pounce when the opportunity presented itself?

That next morning, just before we left for the farm, God used
Tina to totally break me. Pride mixed with shame had kept me
from asking for forgiveness for abusing Tina and terrorizing
Margie and Paula. When little Tina told me that she had filled
that empty Golden Box with kisses just for me, it was like the

final blow that a woodsman delivers as he chops down a proud and towering tree. My pride toppled and I wound up on my knees, begging forgiveness from Tina, as well as Margie and Paula.

Our drive down to the Fishback farm at Tillsonburg that day was perfect in every way. We rolled along recently plowed highways, talking about how wonderful it would be at Grandma and Grandpa's. We could taste that turkey already, and after a steady diet of pabulum, it was going to taste mighty good!

We turned off the main highway onto a country road that took us the several remaining miles to the long driveway up to the Fishback farm. As we came up that last half mile, I was struck by the Currier and Ives scene before me: drifted white snow-banks gleaming in bright sunshine, trees coated with ice and snow, and the hundred-year-old farmhouse on the knoll up ahead seeming to say, "You've come home for Christmas! Welcome! There is only love here!"

It was, without question, the greatest Christmas our family had ever had. All of Margie's brothers and sisters were there with their spouses and children. Tina and Paula joyfully joined their cousins, and their shrieks of laughter rang in the frosty air as they frolicked in the snow, making "angels" and sliding down the long hill in front of the house on sleds that Grandpa always had handy.

On Christmas Day we ate like kings from the bounty of the Fishback farm, which even boasted a grove of maple trees that yielded delicious maple syrup in the spring. Mom Fishback always made plenty of maple sugar candy and had it on hand for Christmas, as well as the fruits of her voluminous canning labors—everything from canned corn to pickled beets, from strawberry jams to cherry preserves.

Mr. Fishback farmed four hundred acres, and in addition to his huge herd of prize dairy cattle, he raised sheep, horses, and pigs. About the only thing he hadn't raised for our Christmas dinner were the pair of twenty-pound-plus turkeys he had purchased nearby.

If Mom and Dad Fishback or any of Margie's brothers and sisters suspected we were having problems, no one said anything. We simply said that we'd been very busy and decided to stop traveling to the U.S. and concentrate on our ministry in Ontario.

"Oh, that means you'll be home more, Paul," said Mom Fishback. "That's important now that the girls are getting bigger."

"You're right, Mom," I agreed, as Margie and I exchanged a knowing look. "I was getting tired of all that traveling anyway."

We stayed at the farm throughout the week and didn't get home until early in January. As we drove up to our house in Don Mills, I wondered how we could possibly keep it. Now we were back to reality, and the stack of bills was bigger than ever. I had sold about all the magic equipment I could, and we still hadn't gotten any checks from the churches that owed us money.

"We'll just trust God, Paul," Margie said. "He'll honor our faith."

And he did. In less than a week, several of the churches paid us, and by the end of the month, all of the checks had arrived. An additional serendipity was a report from Bruce, the young man we left in charge of film rentals after dismissing the others. There had been an unexpected flurry of film requests for Watch Night services on New Year's Eve, and those checks came in as well. We supplemented this with a few substitute teaching jobs that Margie took and a few speaking engagements I took in the immediate area on weekends. In all, we had enough money to get us through the winter and into the spring.

But by Eastertime we again faced the fact that our film business was really in decline. Chuck Peterman had continued to contact me, and he finally offered to come out to Toronto from Gospel Films' home offices in Michigan to help negotiate the sale of our film business to Evangelical Publishers Bookstore, where I had worked in the 1960s.

With the good counsel and help of Chuck Peterman and his wife, Helen, we sold our business to EP, making a deal that bailed us out of almost all our financial difficulties. I was paid the sum of one dollar for the business, based on the agreement that EP would pay off all our creditors, which included several film companies and private parties who had loaned us considerable amounts of money.

Then, two weeks after the sale was completed, I got an unexpected bonus. A. J. Stewart, the EP manager who had given me a break years before, had died, and the new manager knew little about film rentals. In fact, the film rental department at EP had been operating on a reduced basis for several years. Now with the new effort to increase film rental income, he needed help. So he hired me back to manage the business on a salaried basis. Margie also helped, doing part-time work as a bookkeeper, and for the next seven years we worked for EP as well as continuing our ministry throughout Canada and parts of the upper United States.

Using a film on *Pilgrim's Progress* for inspiration, Margie and I developed an entire one-week program on the "Armor of God," which became one of our basic presentations for many years to follow. Each night was devoted to a different part of the armor: the belt of truth, the breastplate of righteousness, shoes able to make you swift to share God's Good News with others, the shield of faith to stop Satan's fiery arrows, the helmet of salvation to protect the brain—which must be always learning more about Christ, and the sword of the Spirit—the Word of God— which must be memorized and understood.

The program included everything: sword drills to involve the children, gospel magic illusions that served as object lessons, hand puppets, and even ventriloquism. As a tiny girl, Tina had become enthralled with ventriloquists and their dolls and asked us to buy her a little "vent doll" while we were passing through Merlin's Castle at Disneyland. She played with little Cindy constantly, making believe she was throwing her voice as she manipulated the doll to nod its head, roll its eyes, and smile.

Later, while we were still traveling in the U.S. and doing amusement park appearances, Tina met Shari Lewis, a well-known professional ventriloquist and entertainer, who encouraged her to keep working with her doll. By the time she was five or six years old, Tina had become a surprisingly good ventriloquist, despite the fact that she couldn't read any books about it and she could only learn by imitating ventriloquists she saw during our travels. She became part of our "Armor of God" presentation. Later her younger sister Paula, who didn't want to be left out, got into the ventriloquism act as well with a doll we bought her named Heather.

Margie and I often laugh together about how different "accidents" and "misunderstandings" led us into our ministry to children. In Timmins, Ontario, a misprint on a flyer brought more five- to twelve-year-olds to watch and listen to my magic acts than the fifteen- to twenty-one-year-olds who were supposed to come. In Toronto I ran across some children at the zoo "by accident," and I also met those small children outside the Fish

Net Youth Club "quite by chance," or so it seemed at the time.

We know that God arranged all those "chance happenings," and in 1975 he arranged another one to expand my tools and my vision for reaching kids more effectively. I had been invited to do a week of meetings at the Onward Gospel Church in Verdun, Quebec, a suburb of Montreal. Carl Crate, whom I had known when he had a church back in Ontario, was the pastor. He called me, saying he had heard about my "Gospel Magic with a Message" presentations and asking if I could come to Verdun to conduct a kids' crusade for an entire week.

What he did not tell me was that in a similar week of meetings the year before, the kids had loved a ventriloquist named Frank Wellington. Carl simply assumed that I knew something about ventriloquism, which was often part of Gospel Magic presentations at that time. All I knew about ventriloquism was what I had seen my tiny daughter doing as she "played" with her doll, Cindy.

Margie, Tina, and Paula all stayed home, and I arrived in Verdun and started on Saturday afternoon with my trademark trick, getting out of a straight jacket in less that twenty-five seconds. No one asked me about ventriloquism that day, but Sunday morning, when I presented Gospel Magic for the entire Sunday school, some of the children came up afterward and wanted to know, "Where's your dummy? We want to talk to your dummy!"

I tried to explain that I only did puppets, but that didn't satisfy the kids. Puppets were OK, but they remembered Frank Wellington and his dummy from the year before, and they wanted more of the same!

Sunday night we packed the church again with the Gospel Magic presentation, but it bothered me when I couldn't deliver what the children kept asking for: "Where's your dummy?" And I was tired of hearing the Catholic kids who had come to the meeting tell me, "They promised us you'd have a dummy—Protestants are liars!"

If only Margie and the girls had come with me, then Tina and Paula could have done some of their ventriloquist routines with their dolls, but there was no point in wallowing around in "if onlys." I had to get out of this on my own—with God's help.

On Monday I started phoning around, trying to find anyone in Montreal who might have a ventriloquist doll I could buy or borrow, but I had no luck.

In desperation, I called a magic shop in New York City and learned that there was one doll for sale—a little guy named TJ, which stood for Timmy Jimmy. I told the proprietor to hold TJ for me and I'd be down to pick him up the next day.

Immediately after finishing the regular three o'clock program for the children, I jumped into a car with two older youths from the church. We drove for almost seven hours to reach New York City by late that night. We slept in the car and were at the door of the magic shop when it opened early the next morning.

As I gave the proprietor the money for little TJ, he said, "Do you vent?"

"Am I a real ventriloquist? No, not really."

The man laughed and said, "This may come in handy then," and he tossed me a little booklet entitled *How to Pull the String.* All the way back to Montreal, as the two collegians took turns at the wheel, I read the booklet and tried to practice operating my new friend, TJ, a little plastic character with red hair who looked like a leprechaun.

As we drove along, all of us were feeling giddy from not having much sleep, and we started to brainstorm about how I might use TJ that evening back at the church. One of my young friends suggested, "Most of the kids speak French as well as English. Why not have TJ speak French?" I laughed and said, "One good reason is because I don't speak French!"

"I do," my friend said. "Why not make TJ smarter than you?"

Before we rolled up to the door, we had it all worked out. I would go out on the stage to the pulpit area while my friend would conceal himself behind a screen a few feet away. He could whisper phrases in French without being heard by the front rows full of kids.

We got back at a few minutes to three, and I quickly shaved and changed clothes before dashing to the stage to perform by 3:15, as scheduled. Just before going on, I prayed, cried a few tears out of sheer terror, and prayed some more. Then I stepped onto the stage with TJ in my arms, much to the delight of the big crowd of children who were waiting for me.

TJ said hello to the crowd and announced that he had heard that I needed a dummy and that he had come to help me out. Then he turned and said to me, "Are you a dummy, or are you looking for a dummy?"

The kids laughed, and I replied, "Well, I might be. Are you a dummy?"

TJ cocked his leprechaun head and said, "What do I look like, your brother?" Then in French, which had been whispered to me by my young friend behind the screen, TJ told the kids, *"I'm* not the dummy. *He's* the one playing with dolls!"

That broke the place up, and we continued the routine with TJ talking to me first in English and then slipping in sly little remarks in French that I "couldn't understand." Fortunately I have instantaneous recall, so when my friend whispered the words in French to me, I could remember them long enough to repeat them. Seconds later, however, I had totally forgotten what had been said.

The kids loved the entire presentation, even though I moved my lips quite a bit. There was nothing I could do. You don't learn ventriloquism in one seven-hour drive. I decided I might as well confront my "weakness" head-on, and as the routine ended I had TJ throw in the punch line: "Well, if you don't understand what I'm saying, just read *his* lips!"

TJ was a howling success from the start. I used him through-out the rest of the week and got him into dialogue with the audience when the kids would ask him questions. It was the beginning of my ventriloquist career, which became a vital part of our ministry to children.

When I got back home, Margie and the girls were thrilled with my acquisition of TJ and my new interest in ventriloquism. The girls gave me all the tips they could because, even at the ages of seven and five, they knew a lot more about throwing their voices than I did.

A little later I picked up another doll named Rusty at a very reasonable price. Rusty was larger than TJ, with more moving parts and better expressions. For awhile I used both dolls on occasion, but eventually I concentrated on perfecting different routines with Rusty. Tina and Paula kept helping me, but I always felt a little bit unsure of myself.

The following April, Redd Harper called with some interesting news: "Padnah, we're organizing a tour of Israel, and we want to include some people who can give a gospel witness—sort of informally. There's a law against proselytin' in Israel, so what-ever we do has to look like part of a tour group. Are you in-terested?"

I had never been to Israel and, after talking it over with Margie, decided to go on the tour while she remained in Toronto with the girls. A group of over sixty people flew to Israel for the tour, which included an evangelism team that had to operate "without portfolio," giving brief impromptu programs at night in hotel dining rooms or in the daytime near villages located close to tourist sites.

Included in our team were Redd and Laura Harper; Phil and Louie Palermo, who sang; and Jeannette Clift George, the actress who played Corrie ten Boom in *The Hiding Place,* who gave her testimony.

I was there to do gospel magic for children, and I soon discovered that the Israeli kids liked Rusty better than any of my tricks! I still wasn't really professional with Rusty, but he drew the kids in droves anyway.

Our tour group spent almost three weeks in Israel, traveling through all the well-known biblical sites and sharing the gospel in an informal way. It was this trip to Israel that really gave me the experience I needed to get much more proficient with handling a "vent doll," as they were called in the trade. By the time Rusty and I got back, we were a real team, and he became more and more a part of my gospel presentations through the fall and winter.

When I got back to Toronto in early May, I redoubled my efforts at EP, trying to line up all the film rentals I could to make a good impression on my employers. I also was doing children's crusade meetings at night. That meant I would have to finish work at five o'clock, dash home, gulp some food, and be back at church by seven o'clock ready to go. The Ontario Sunday School Convention was coming up at People's Church in Toronto, and I was scheduled for three lectures and a spot on the main program.

I had been pushing myself far too hard, running on pure adrenaline. On Friday, just before the Sunday School Convention was to open, I was rushing down the stairs at home to get a piece of equipment when another stress attack knocked me completely cold. I woke up in the North York General Hospital. The pain was as bad as ever, but as soon as I heard the words *stress attack,* I knew I'd get through it.

I spent several days in the hospital and was allowed to go back to work with strict orders to cut back and take it easy. Unfortunately, I've never been very good at cutting back. Summer arrived, and Margie and I took our usual two-month leave of absence from EP in July and August to do vacation Bible school programs in the area. The film business was slow then, so the arrangement worked out nicely.

Because of overscheduling that I had done months before, Margie and I found ourselves covering three different vacation Bible schools in one day, one in the morning, one right after lunch, and one in the evening.

We had a little camping trailer that we would park in a central location close to all the churches where we would be teaching. Tina, who was eight at the time, went along with Margie and me and took part in the programs. By then she had become a skilled ventriloquist and was much better at not moving her mouth than I would ever be. Five-year-old Paula would stay back at the trailer with a baby-sitter, playing with her favorite toy, a creche set made out of olive wood, which I had purchased at a bargain price just outside of Tiberius in Israel.

Paula loved to talk to Mary, Joseph, Baby Jesus, the wise men, and the other characters that made up the set. She was always happy, perky, and seemed content, so Margie and I didn't think much of leaving her behind with the sitter when we went off to cover our VBS appointments each day.

One day, just after lunch, we had to double back to the trailer to pick up some equipment I had forgotten. There was Paula, under a tree, playing with her creche set as usual. As I walked by I said hi and then inquired, "Honey, where are Mary and Joseph? I don't see them."

"Oh, it's OK, Daddy," Paula replied. "Mary and Joseph are off on a crusade, and the three wise men are baby-sitting Jesus."

I stopped dead in my tracks and did a double take: "The three wise men are baby-sitting Jesus?"

"Oh, it's OK, Dad. Mary and Joseph are just like you and Mama —they're always gone."

I smiled and told Paula I loved her, gave her a kiss, and went back to the car where Margie and Tina were waiting. I told Margie what Paula had said, and at first we laughed about it. Later, however, the impact of my five-year-old daughter's words, uttered without rancor in childish innocence, hit me hard: *"Mary and Joseph are just like you and Mama—they're always gone."* Later that evening, after finishing our final VBS meeting, Margie and I went for a walk and I mentioned again what Paula had said. "Maybe the Lord is using Paula to get our attention.

Maybe he's telling us to 'be still and know that I am God.'

"And you know, Margie," I continued, "we're extra busy this summer, not just because we want to minister, but because the pay is better."

Margie gave me one of her knowing smiles. "I think I know what you mean, Paul, but just to be sure, how do you define 'better pay'?"

"Well, last summer we covered this same area but only did two churches, and we would usually get one hundred dollars a day in love offerings. But this summer, by getting to three different churches, our offerings are up around two hundred dollars a day. That's why I took the extra appointments."

"Paul, that's right. I knew it was happening, too, but I wanted the extra money just as much as you did. I think it's time to talk about changing our ways."

Ironically, we had always made a big point to parents in our meetings "to have enough time for your kids," and now out of the mouths of one of our own babes had come the truth: Paul Powers and his wife were always busy, off on crusades! That summer Margie and I decided to practice what we preached. We established special Family Nights, scheduling nothing else and letting the girls choose whatever they wanted—a favorite restaurant, favorite food they wanted, games they liked to play, television programs they preferred to watch (with a little guidance from us, of course).

Having special Family Nights has been our policy right up to the present. Today Tina and Paula are both in college, but they still get home much of the time, and we still have Family Nights. The only difference now is, they not only pick their favorite foods, they help cook them!

Since quitting the secular magic circuit in 1971, our ministry to children has occupied our lives, but it has never shoved our own daughters from the center of our love and concern. As they grew up, Tina and Paula joined us in ministry, but only because they wanted to, never because Daddy or Mommy wanted to use them or show them off.

There are all kinds of ways to abuse a child, and I'm often reminded of the words of the apostle Paul, who spoke of keeping himself under control "so that after I have preached to others, I myself will not be disqualified for the prize" (1 Corinthians 9:27, NIV).

God forbid that families should wind up "castaways" on the barren islands of busyness, or that their children should be abused or neglected. Unfortunately, it happens much too often. As we have gone from church to church, camp to camp, and town to town throughout the world, we have seen thousands of children who know the same kind of pain LaVern felt as a small boy. In the next chapter, I want to tell you a few of their stories.

EIGHTEEN
ANDY AND
THE LITTLE PEOPLE

LOST
"RUSTY"
Ventriloquist's Doll
Reward
No Questions Asked

That was the ad I ran in Toronto newspapers after Rusty was
kidnapped one cold wintry day, just after I finished a program at
Sick Children's Hospital in Toronto. I took all the equipment out
to the parking lot. I left it sitting by the van while I went back
inside to pick up Tina and Paula, who had come along to help
me. When we got back to the van and I went around to the back
to put the different cases in the trunk, Rusty was gone.

Despite reporting the theft of Rusty to the police and running
ads in the paper, not a single lead ever turned up. It was hard
getting along without Rusty. He had become not only part of my
presentations, but part of me as well, and replacing him would
not be easy. It also would not be cheap. Good vent dolls are
expensive, and I had to start saving what I could to try to buy
another one someday.

And it wasn't simply a matter of taking my first doll, TJ out of
his box and start using him again. I had contributed TJ to Vent
Haven, an internationally known museum for ventriloquist's
dolls. Some of the best-known names in the world are on
display today at Vent Haven, including Charlie McCarthy,
Mortimer Snerd, and Jerry Mahoney.

The following July our entire family went to a convention of ventriloquists and magicians held in Kentucky. There are always dozens of booths at these trade shows, selling all kinds of equipment and services, and I was hoping to find a new vent doll, as were Tina and Paula, who felt that Cindy and Heather were getting too old and too small. They wanted dolls that would have more movement and expression.

We covered every booth where vent dolls were on display, but none of them appealed to any of us. We were about ready to give up our search—at least for the time being—when we met Clinton Detweiler, who directed a ventriloquism school in Toronto. We sat down to have a cup of coffee with Clinton in the hotel cafeteria and began talking with him about what vent dolls were available and what might be coming on the market soon. Paula wandered off a short distance and began watching people around the swimming pool who were "doing vent." Dozens of ventriloquists were at the convention, and they would often gather at the swimming pool with their dolls and practice.

Suddenly Paula dashed back into the cafeteria and exclaimed, "Daddy, Daddy, I've just found the perfect doll for you! And he's for sale!"

Paula proceeded to describe a little boy doll who sounded like the proverbial "perfect kid." We were just finishing our coffee, so we decided to stroll out to the pool and investigate.

"That's him, that's Andy!" Paula chattered excitedly as she pointed to the far end of the pool at what looked like a little boy sunning himself in a chair.

"Paula, that's a real little boy," Margie insisted. "You just can't buy a little boy. . . ."

Paula pulled at our hands, insisting, "No, Mommy, he's not a little boy. He's a doll, and he's for sale!"

We walked over toward the "little boy," who sat motionless in a chair, seeming to enjoy the sun on his face. As we got closer, we could see that he was a doll. Just then Clinton Detweiler said, "Oh, I know whose doll that is. And Paula's right—he's up for sale."

The doll's owner had just sprayed him with a coat of lacquer and was sitting nearby waiting for the doll to dry. But he was also interested in trying to make a sale—at an astronomical price.

When I got a good look at the doll, my heart immediately

said, *This is the perfect kid for Sunday school, VBS, crusades—everywhere!* Margie was having practically the same thoughts. All three of them, Margie, Tina, and Paula, kept urging, "Daddy . . . he's the *ONE!*"

I asked the doll's owner if it was definitely for sale, and he said, "Oh, yes, of course—pick him up . . . his name is Greg."

"No, it isn't," Paula insisted, "it's Andy. I named him!"

As I slid my right hand up Andy's back and cradled him in the palm of my left, the effect was incredible! The way he fit, the way he responded, even the voice I gave him just for a tryout—everything was perfect. It was as if I had put on a custom-made glove, designed only for me! I knew I had to have Andy, despite the high price. As I negotiated with his owner, it looked hopeless until Clinton stepped in and offered to loan me part of the money. I finally made a deal, and Andy was ours! Later I thanked Clinton fervently for helping me out, and he said, "Glad to do it . . . Andy is an abused doll, you know."

I didn't know, and Clinton filled me in on how Andy had been quite famous in his day. One of his former owners had used him on an early television show out of Los Angeles—a program called, "Hi, Kids!"

But his owner started using drugs and alcohol, lost his Los Angeles television job and wound up in Nashville performing at the Grand Ol' Opry. One night after a show, Andy's owner went into a drunken rage, smashing him against the wall, ripping off both of his legs and one of his arms. When the man finally sobered up and saw what he had done to Andy, he had him repaired, and later decided to put him up for sale at the upcoming convention. That's where we found Andy, and after we bought him we discovered there was still a lot of repair work to be done.

First we took him back to our hotel room, screwed off his head and washed the rest of him thoroughly in the tub. (Today Andy often tells audiences that he's "a Baptist, but only from the neck down!")

In his old life as "Greg," Andy had used cigarettes and alcohol as part of the act with his owner. We removed drinking and sucking mechanisms that were corroded with liquor and nicotine, and we also took out another gadget which had enabled Greg to spit on the audience, which his partner had him do from time to time in an attempt to get laughs. On the following Sunday, while doing a program in a church in Detroit, we had Andy dedicated as the Lord's instrument for ministry, vowing never to treat him as a toy.

We also had to do extensive repair work on Andy's face, which was still chipped and scratched in several places. And we had to fix one of his legs and one of his arms because some of the springs were broken. All in all, it took another five hundred dollars to put Andy in top shape, but it was worth every penny and much more.

As we worked on Andy, the parallels between his life and mine were obvious. As is the case with most ventriloquists, I grew very close to my new little friend. Andy's predecessors, TJ and Rusty, were valuable, but Andy became invaluable. He was the final touch in revolutionizing our ministry and giving us a new medium that would be more effective with children than illusions and tricks.

After I had the stress attack, the doctors warned me not to do my escape-from-the-straight-jacket trick anymore. It put too much pressure on certain areas of my chest and could easily trigger another incident. Andy became my new trademark or "grabber" to gain attention and interest. Having Andy also helped me get away from having to describe myself as a "gospel magician." Instead, I started saying, "ventriloquist and gospel illustrator." That opened up doors to many churches that would otherwise be unwilling to bring in a magician.

Everywhere I appear, Andy is indispensable. He's a natural icebreaker to warm up the crowd because he appeals equally to adults and children. And he's even a big hit when I make occasional visits to college campuses. When Andy does Shakespeare, it brings down the house.

My dialogues with Andy are designed to help children deal with their problems and concerns. He and I will talk about lying and exaggerating—or maybe fears will be the subject. A lot of children are afraid of the dark, and Andy lets them know that he understands because he's afraid of going back in his case and having me shut the lid!

Sometimes Andy will show up in wrap-around sunglasses with his shirt collar turned up, telling everybody he's out to be cool and "with it." It's a natural lead-in on how to resist peer pressure.

On another day Andy may greet me with, "Hi, Chubby!" which

gets a good laugh, but then leads to talking about how you just can't call your friends names if you want to have any real friends.

Perhaps the most effective topic of all is our discussion of abuse. One moment the crowd is roaring at Andy's antics, and the next moment the room is silent when he tells about the time "I got beaten up, too." I've seen adults weeping over Andy's story of how his owner tore him to pieces.

Andy is the perfect lead-in to talk to the many different kids who come to our programs—the cocky and the bold, as well as the shy and fearful who would otherwise never open up. Because we have both been beaten and abused, Andy and I are especially aware of the hurting ones—children like Jennifer, who went into a rage the first time I walked into a room where she was working on a craft at a summer camp. The moment she saw me, she started kicking, screaming, and telling me to "get away!"

As the days went by, I heard of other situations involving this same little girl. In one case, a male counselor in his teens was trying to show her how to play a game and in doing so he brushed against her. She smashed the game to bits, turned around, and whacked him one, screaming, "Don't you touch me!"

I was continuing to share the story of LaVern through the week, and on Wednesday morning, Jennifer ran out of the program and into the bathroom, crying hysterically. My daughter Paula, who was in her teens at the time, went in and started to talk to the little girl and pulled the story out of her. She had been physically and sexually abused since the age of three, first by her father and then by her stepfather. Paula quieted her and prayed with her, and on Wednesday night she sat a few rows closer to the front. Andy and I continued our dialogue.

On Thursday morning Jennifer was one row from the front, and by Thursday night, she had a seat in the front row. She was laughing as hard as anyone at Andy, who had been trying to make friends with her all week. Then she began talking to Andy, completely oblivious to the rest of the people in the room. At one point Andy invited her to come up and shake hands. She did so—a major breakthrough because, after all, Andy is a "little boy," and Jennifer hated anyone male.

On Saturday night during Fireside time, children were given

an opportunity to share what the week had meant. The fourth child to get up was Jennifer. She explained that during the week she had asked Jesus for forgiveness of her sins and had also invited him into her heart. She also said she would pray for her daddy, and now she knew what had happened was "not her fault."

She began to cry softly. Then she looked up and said, "Jesus loves me . . . he loves me now. I am loved and I am wanted. I know my mommy loves me, and she doesn't blame me . . . and now I have a Father who won't hurt me!"

I wish I could say that Jennifer is a rare example, but, unfortunately, she is one of many abused children who turn up in our meetings. I recall a girl who jumped up in the middle of a program screaming, "If God is like my father, I'd rather go to hell!"

But most children let me know their problems much less dramatically, usually by slipping up after the service and saying things like, "Please pray for my daddy because he drinks a lot and he hits me and my mommy, and he's home right now on the couch. Please pray for him."

And then perhaps the mother will come by and I will say, "Your daughter just asked me to pray for her daddy."

And the mother will look up with clouded eyes and ask tensely, *"What did she say to you?"*

When I tell her I usually get one of two reactions: a request for counseling sometime that week, or embarrassment and anger. This whole area of abuse is extremely sensitive, and many adults do not want to talk about it. I've had a father jump up in the middle of a meeting where I was sharing about abused children, shouting that I had no business speaking that way in his church and that I should leave immediately. I've had pastors tell me to "go easy" on this area or not speak of it at all because "our people just don't want to hear that—they want to hear a message from the Bible."

But it is hard to be silent, because the hurting children are all around us. I think of Billy, an Indian lad who had been beaten by his father and passed around from foster home to foster home. But physical abuse was only one of Billy's problems. He came to a camp where I was speaking, and I made friends with him on Tuesday. On the last night of camp he came by to talk after dinner. He wanted to know if I was speaking that night, and I said yes. Then he put his hand on my shoulder, and I put my arm around him. "I love you in Jesus' love," I said.

"I know that . . . I've known it since Tuesday . . . you don't have to tell me."

"But I want you to hear it," I explained.

Billy stared at the ground, not saying anything. Then he looked up and said, with tears in his eyes, "What I'd like to know is why the people in my church don't say that? Why do they just see my color?"

And then there was David who knew plenty about rejection too. Young David could play the piano beautifully, but he was short, awkward, and kind of homely. He was the kind of little boy who often gets labeled a "nerd" by fellow campers. After hearing Andy and me do a dialogue on name-calling and rejection, he sidled up to me during break time and asked, "Are you really a pastor?"

"Yes, I'm an ordained pastor, David," I replied.

"But you don't talk like a pastor, you don't look like a pastor . . ."

"What do I look like?"

David looked up at me, studied my face, and then said, "Like what a Christian looks like in the Bible, I guess."

I gave David a big hug and went back to my cabin, closed the door, and cried. I cried for David and the thousands of kids who need love and acceptance, just as I did when I was his age. God has filled my heart with a love for them all, and I want to help them, to "fix things" for them, just as I fixed Andy. But children who have been abused, rejected, and bruised by life don't fix as easily as a doll made of wood and metal. It takes time and prayer—a lot of prayer.

Soon after becoming a Christian, I was told of the importance of prayer, and throughout my ministry I have always given prayer great value and importance. For many years I believed in prayer because I was knew it was biblical—and the source of a Christian's power. But about a year after getting Andy I had an experience that helped me see prayer in a totally new light.

I was invited to take part in the opening Sunday services at a brand new church in Port Hope, Ontario, just a few miles from the Bowmanville reformatory. I spoke to the entire Sunday school, telling them the story of how LaVern and his fellow inmates at Bowmanville had come to the Christmas program given by the Gideons. I described how LaVern had come up on stage to get his gift only to discover it was a New Testament and how, with curses, he had ripped it up and thrown it back in the man's face.

Then to emphasize my point about how the Word of God can never be destroyed, I did my "Bible Tear" illusion. Afterward I was gathering my equipment and preparing to do another program for the junior church during the next hour when a nicely dressed, elderly lady with bluish white hair walked up.

"I heard you speak during Sunday school," she said. "Do you remember the name of the man who tried to hand LaVern a New Testament that day in the reformatory?" I had to admit that I had never really known his name, but she just smiled and said, "It doesn't make any difference. He was my husband! He died over two years ago, but I want you to know that he brought home that box of Bibles that he never got to give to any of the boys that day. He also saved the one you ripped up, and he prayed over that torn little New Testament for years, asking God to save you!"

Goose bumps rose on the back of my neck, and I hugged her as we wept together. As she left, she handed me a little white package, wrapped in blue ribbon. It was the same kind of package I had ripped open that day at Bowmanville! As she turned away, I heard her say only one word: *"Finally . . ."*

I didn't need any more than that because I knew what she meant. *Finally* God had answered her husband's prayers, and hers. *Finally* she learned that the hostile young boy who had cursed her husband and God's Word had realized what Christmas truly means and had discovered God's endless love!

With prayer it is always so. *Finally,* God answers—in some cases, not for many years. *How* he answers is part of the challenge and mystery of being a Christian. I have often heard it said that the best prayer seeks only God's will, not yours. Jesus modeled that kind of prayer the night before he died: "Not my will, Father, but yours be done."

As the 1970s came to a close, our family tussled with finding God's will concerning one of the most important decisions we would ever make. Our prayers and the way God answered them changed our lives and our entire ministry.

NINETEEN
HOW THE
WEST WON US

"Vancouver, here we come!" I announced as I eased our heavily loaded minivan down the driveway. Tina and Paula, ages twelve and nine, chattered excitedly in the backseat while Margie sat beside me, pensive and thoughtful.

The huge moving van, loaded with our furniture and other belongings, had already pulled out. I had made a final inspection of the empty house, and now it was time to leave Don Mills, our home for thirteen years. It was the end of July 1980, and we were headed not only into a new decade, but a new life.

"Vancouver, British Columbia! It's so far, Paul, will our little van make it?"

"It has to make it," I said cheerfully. "I have to be ready to go to work out there by August 4, and we have to be ready when the moving van comes. Besides, Margie, you've been saying that this is our Macedonian Call. God wouldn't call us and then have us break down, would he?"

Margie laughed and settled back for the twenty-five-hundred-mile drive. What else could she do? We had made our decision, sold our house, and could only trust that this move fit into God's will, which we had been so carefully seeking.

It had all started a year before when my cousin called and told us his church in Vancouver wanted to have us come out for two weeks of meetings. We accepted his invitation and took Tina and Paula along, planning to spend two weeks but remaining for three as the people in his church gave us an enthusiastic welcome and response. While we were in Vancouver, we toured the city and saw that it was in the midst of a building boom with many housing tracts and new churches being built to serve the thousands who were arriving each year.

We returned to Toronto, wondering if perhaps British Columbia was a new "mission field" we should investigate further. Besides, as the seventies had drawn to a close, Margie and I talked frequently about the danger of "getting stale" in our ministry. For almost fifteen years we had been going to the same churches and camps throughout eastern Canada, year after year, using basically the same messages and the same routines. Perhaps it was time for a change, a completely new scene. But was that God speaking or only our own human logic?

"Margie, I don't want to move to British Columbia just because we think we might be getting a little stale here in Ontario. There has to be more reason than that!"

"Well, why don't we put the house up for sale as a fleece and see what happens," Margie suggested. "Let's pray and leave it in God's hands. If the house sells immediately, we'll take that as a sign he wants us to move. If it doesn't, we'll wait."

Our house went on the market in September with a sixty-day listing and we got very few lookers and no offers. We shelved the idea of moving and kept praying, asking God to show us his will. Our fleece had come up dry, but we still kept feeling that God wanted us to do more than just part-time ministry to children. Full-time ministry in Ontario had never seemed like an option because there were already over a dozen full-time children's evangelists working throughout Ontario and eastern Canada. On the other hand, we knew of not one in British Columbia. But if we were to go to British Columbia, why hadn't God found a buyer for our house, even during the so-called "off season" when real estate moves slowly?

We were pulled this way and that. We had a lot of "competition" in Ontario, but at the same time it was safe and familiar ground, and we had developed a following of people who liked our ministry. On the other hand, we did have those feelings of getting a bit stale.

One argument for moving was that Ontario's winters were long and cold and had really been getting harder on my health. I had been catching walking pneumonia about twice every year. On the other hand, how could we support ourselves in

British Columbia until we got established in a full-time ministry?

Feeling like Tevye in *Fiddler on the Roof*—as we looked from one hand to the other—we went through the winter and into the spring, still praying and waiting for some clear direction. In May I was invited to attend a conference for Baptist pastors from throughout eastern Canada, held in Mary Lake, Ontario, north of Toronto. While at the conference I talked to friends who were planning to move to British Columbia soon. They considered BC the "new frontier" of ministry in Canada, and I agreed. As I shared our family's experience in Vancouver, I concluded, "The place is booming—what potential for ministry!"

"You've got that missionary look in your eye, Paul," said one of my pastor friends. "Why don't we pray with you and ask for the peace that God promises?" Several of us did pray together, and while it made me feel better, I still wasn't sure about what we should do. The next day I phoned Margie: "How do you feel about British Columbia? Are you still for it?"

"Yes, Paul, I've been thinking and praying, and I still believe it's the way God could open the door for us to go into full-time ministry. The potential is there; all we need is the faith."

"There's an awful lot to think about . . . leaving the home where the girls have lived all their lives . . . leaving an established ministry that we do have, even though it is part-time . . ."

"Well, Paul, if we're ever going to make a change with the girls, this is as good a time as any with Paula still fairly young and Tina headed into junior high in the fall. She'll have to be switching schools anyway. My main concern is how we can support ourselves—at least at the beginning until we become known in the area."

"I'll call Dr. Peter Allinger in Vancouver and see if he still needs a sales representative," I said as we hung up. Immediately I dialed Peter, who was president of International Audio Visual and Faith Films, Ltd., a film rental and supply company in Vancouver. When I told him we were interested in moving west, his booming voice was enthusiastic. "Paul, your timing's perfect! If you can move out this summer, I can put you to work immediately doing promotion work for the new Dobson film series. And, of course, you will be sales rep for all of the other products we handle."

There seemed to be only one thing left to do—try that same fleece that had failed seven months before. We put our house on the market in May . . . and it sold by the end of June!

I quickly phoned Peter Allinger to tell him the news. "Great!" he said. "Why don't we get you involved by having you represent us at the Christian Film Distributors Convention in Texas? We'll fly you out."

I attended that meeting and got back to Toronto just in time to help Margie finish packing. We left on a hot afternoon in late July and arrived in Vancouver on August 4. All the way across Canada we got continual assurances that God was leading. Almost every day there was an opportunity to talk to people about the Lord and, in some instances, lead them to Christ. In every instance, we never sought these opportunities; the people approached us.

One of my first responsibilities with International Audio Visual was to travel from town to town in Vancouver, setting up "premiere showings" of the Focus on the Family film series, featuring Dr. James Dobson. I would go into a community, arrange for a complimentary showing of the film in a local church or high school gymnasium, and then take orders from pastors and others who were interested in renting the film for use in their churches or in other ministry settings.

During our first three years in British Columbia, I concentrated on my full-time job with International Audio Visual but also took opportunities to establish our ministry to children. As I traveled from church to church doing film premieres and other sales representative work, I would occasionally present a program for children to "test the waters." I wanted to be sure that the warm enthusiasm we had experienced in 1979 wasn't some kind of fluke, and I learned a lot.

I soon realized that believers in British Columbia were more conservative than those in Ontario and Quebec. Back east, our approach to children's meetings and crusades had been snappy, humorous, and packed with action. I hadn't been in Vancouver very long when a young pastor named Bill Henley took me aside and said frankly, "Paul, your program is great, but it's too 'razzamatazzy.' You need to pull it together tighter and concentrate on getting more biblical depth."

I was grateful for Bill's advice and quickly got together with Margie to make changes in our programs. We didn't mind adjusting the programs, as long as we didn't have to compromise our message. And since churches in British Columbia apparently wanted more Bible, not less, we would be happy to oblige! Bill Henley has been our dear friend ever since we came to British Columbia, and I'm thankful for the day that he talked to me, "eyeball to eyeball," and told me the truth.

As part of our fresh new start in British Columbia we designed a program with a western theme, heavy on evangelism. We totally revamped our "Armor of God" presentation and also did several new programs: "Here Comes Jesus" shared stories from the life of our Lord; a new missions program was designed to give adults, particularly, a heart for children; and a new program on the "Fruit of the Spirit" stressed "knowing, growing, and showing."

British Columbia was the perfect proving ground for my vision of a little children's army that would rise up out of our current generation not only to know Christ, but to serve him. Years before, I had dreamed one night of children from the ghettos of Toronto and the slums of Sarnia, as well as the comfortable homes of Don Mills. I'm sure the dream was prompted by my memories of a painting I had seen at the Forest Lawn Memorial Park in Glendale, California. In "The Resurrection," the artist depicted the open tomb and a guardian angel ready to tell Jesus' disciples, "He has risen!" But the reason the painting stuck in my mind was that army of faces in the sky— seemingly thousands of people of every age, race, and color— representing the untold millions who would believe in the risen Savior.

In my dream I saw the faces of abused children who were stepping forward without fear or terror to tell their parents about the Savior's love. They could no longer sit silently, being told to be seen but not heard. This army of small children, motivated by the love of Jesus, would carry God's banner throughout the world.

I repeatedly discussed my dream with Margie, and out of those talks came the concept of H.I.T.—Helpers In Training. Our goal with H.I.T. is to develop a three-year program with a church, starting with children ages nine and ten, and trying to get back every year to give them further training.

On the first night of a crusade, I meet early with interested children. We have a light supper, followed by a period of intensive instruction in how to be ushers, help keep order with smaller children, distribute materials, run slide and film projectors—

even how to repair broken film, just as I learned to do when I was ten years old. Later, during the meeting, the H.I.T. children get to apply what they have learned in a hands-on way.

By the middle of the week, these kids are running Bible quizzes and sword drills, helping lead songs, and, in some cases, trying out the rudiments of ventriloquism. With Tina and Paula's help, I have introduced dozens of young people to ventriloquism over the years—many of whom have gone on to buy dolls of their own.

One of the key concepts behind H.I.T. is to help children learn accountability and responsibility—how to be Christian leaders. We want them to go beyond the week of fun and inspiration while "Uncle Paul" is in town. We want them to grow, and we work with the Christian education people at the church to help them keep developing and learning all year long. We even provide a manual that contains assignments they can fill out and pages where they can record their progress and personal observations about what they're learning.

All of our programs went over well in British Columbia, and by 1983 Margie and I were both feeling a strong pull to try to get away from working in Christian film rentals and go full-time into children's ministry. But the laws of British Columbia were plain: we would have to organize a nonprofit association, complete with a board of directors, a charter, and a budget. While we were thinking about how to accomplish all that, we heard about Amsterdam '83, an international convention of itinerant evangelists, scheduled to be held in Amsterdam, Holland, in May. I called Redd Harper and asked him if he was going. He said, "Yes. Would you, Margie, and the children like to go?"

"Oh, of course, it would be terrific, but I'm afraid it would be too expensive to fly us all over there. And then there would be the problem of where to stay, the food, and all the rest of it."

"Wa'll, padnah, let me see what I can do," said Redd. "I'll call you back soon."

When Redd called back, he had arranged with World Wide Pictures to give us some financial assistance to go to Amsterdam '83. With that money, plus some loans from friends, we made the trip.

Amsterdam '83 was a two-week long convention held in giant Rie Auditorium near downtown Amsterdam. Thousands of delegates came from all over the world to hear hundreds of the top Christian speakers of the day, including Billy Graham, Josh McDowell, Luis Palau, and Paul Cho, pastor of the huge Full Gospel Central Church of Seoul, Korea, with a congregation of over 150,000 members.

The theme for the convention was "To Do the Work of an Evangelist." For two solid weeks we had a steady diet of messages, seminars, and workshops all designed to challenge us to live a life of faith, trusting God for everything. We stayed in an apartment in The Hague, a town some fifty miles from Amsterdam, which meant long rides back and forth each day on the train.

While commuting, Margie and I had long discussions about how I might leave International Audio Visual and concentrate on a full-time ministry to children. We kept asking ourselves, "What is our faith really made of?" My failures of past years had taught me many lessons, but would it all make any difference? Was it worth the risk, or would I fail again?

On Saturday night, as the convention came to a close, there was a showing of the new Billy Graham film *The Prodigal,* a story of a young boy who wandered far from his family and his faith, only to be drawn back later through God's loving patience. As the curtain went down, Dr. Tom Houston stepped to the microphone and invited all those who wished to make a new commitment of their ministry to come forward.

I stood to my feet, turned to Margie and said, "God is speaking to me . . . I really feel he wants us to go full-time in ministry and really launch out."

Margie stood up and said, "Are you asking us *all?*"

"No, I'm the one who must take the step, but I would like your support."

Margie hugged me and kissed me, and we started toward the front. We hadn't even gotten out of our row, however, when Tina grabbed my arm and said, "We want to follow you, Daddy."

I turned to her and said, "But darling, you girls aren't part of the ministry."

Tina didn't argue—she just said, matter-of-factly, "Yes, we are!"

I looked at my daughters for a long moment. There was Tina, fifteen, and Paula, twelve—their eyes shining and their faces glowing with a look that would not be denied. I said, "Yes . . . yes, of course you are! C'mon!"

They hugged us, and we all joined hands and went to the

front along with hundreds of other pastors, evangelists, and Christian workers from countries throughout the world who had stepped forward to say, "We really mean business with God." Many of these people were poor, and they had sacrificed a great deal to make the trip. Some had sold their goats or their pigs, or whatever they owned, to scrape together enough money for the journey to Amsterdam.

Tina and Paula had made friends with some missionaries from Nairobi, Kenya, and South Africa during the week. The girls had their ventriloquist dolls with them, and their new African friends became fascinated with "how to make them talk." Before the week was out, Tina and Paula had given Cindy and Heather to the African missionaries, explaining, "Daddy, they can't get anything like this in their country." I was happy to see the girls make this gesture of love and generosity, but I warned them, "You know this means you'll have no dolls at all, and I don't know when we can afford to get new ones."

"That's OK, Daddy," said Tina. "We've wanted new dolls for a long time so we can do a better job. We'll just trust God and see what happens. But right now we want these people to have Cindy and Heather."

Amsterdam '83 gave our family a charge that sent us so high, we still haven't come down. We returned to British Columbia determined to follow through in establishing a full-time non-profit ministry to children. By fall, Little People's Ministry Association was born.

The first board of directors included mostly people from the Vancouver area whom I had met in churches and who had a love and appreciation for children. They included Bill O'Connor, an engineer; Leroy Gager, a Bible college professor; Cam Moore, an elementary schoolteacher; Ron Harry, an accountant; and Trevor Newton, purchasing agent for the Bayshore Hotels.

Not only did our family have a brand new full-time ministry, but we got two new "children" to boot! Shortly after returning from Amsterdam '83, we were all doing a camp on Vancouver Island, and a lady asked me if Tina and Paula did ventriloquism.

"Yes, they are excellent ventriloquists, but right now they're without dolls because they gave them away in Europe."

The woman, a member of the prominent Knight family of Victoria, B.C., came back a few minutes later and handed me a check for five hundred dollars. "This is to help find new dolls for Tina and Paula," Mrs. Knight said, and she walked away.

Immediately I contacted a friend who was an expert in vent dolls. I gave him the money as a down payment, told him what Tina and Paula were looking for, and in about six weeks, Diana and Ashley arrived. Both dolls were almost as professional in quality as Andy, and at last the girls had equipment worthy of their skills. The girls became an even more important part of our programming for kids' crusades and camps, and they developed presentations of professional quality, with perfect timing and absolutely no movement of the lips.

In fact, they became so professional that they let me know that they didn't want to appear on stage with Andy and me. Kindly but firmly they told me, "Daddy, you move your lips, and it makes us look bad." That policy has held throughout the years, and even today, although Andy and I may introduce Paula and Diana, or Tina and Ashley, we then step off the stage.

Since Little People's Ministry became a reality in 1983, we have had the privilege of traveling throughout the world to minister to young children. I've gone back alone to hold meetings in Egypt as well as Israel, and our entire family has been to the Arctic and to almost every state in the Union. Paula and I were in Mexico right after the huge earthquake in 1987, and in 1989 we all traveled to Australia and New Zealand to hold several weeks of meetings. We look forward to going to the Philippines sometime in 1990.

I'm often asked what drives me. Why do I keep putting myself under the stress of continual travel, constantly having to get reenergized for another week of meetings somewhere else? My first answer is that my energy comes from Jesus Christ who found a young man who had been physically and mentally abused as a child, who had become a thief and a murderer and, later, a hate-filled convict who only wanted revenge, particularly on his father. Christ changed all that, and he continued to change and mold me as I became an adult. He gave me the finest wife and daughters any man could ask for, and he showed me that the path of materialism and pleasure-seeking may be brightly lit but is full of traps and chuck holes.

God let me squeeze myself into a corner so small that I had no place to hide, and I had to admit my weaknesses and deal with the sin in my life. It's easy to talk about weaknesses and faults; it is much harder to admit sin, but that's what disobedience, greed, carelessness, and hypocrisy are. You miss God's mark, going your way, not his.

Fueling my passion for ministry is my love for children, which at times is almost overwhelming. I suppose it starts with my love for my own daughters. I still have that Golden Box, "blown full of kisses" by a little girl who forgave her daddy for slapping her so brutally, only wanting him to know that she loved him very much. On days when life seems too tough to handle, I take out that box and feel its love. It has become a symbol to me of the love that little children are always ready to share with anyone who cares for them. When I see that box, I see hurting children all over the world, many of them hurting just as badly as I once hurt, suffering as I suffered. I feel compelled to reach as many as I can with the love of Jesus.

One other dynamic also drives me on. It is the memory of my father, the monster who smashed and stomped me the day my mother died, the sadist who beat me bloody with a rubber hose, the cold, uncaring parent who told a reform school director, "Send him to hell!"

At one time I would have given anything to kill my father—I hated him that much. But God changed my heart, and, unbelievably, he changed my father's heart as well. My ministry to children today is built upon my unwavering belief that no matter how desperate life can be, there is always hope. In the final chapter I will tell you why.

TWENTY
"It's OK, Paul ... I Love You!"

"Hello, Lambert? . . . Paul Powers . . . It's good to hear your voice too. I'm hoping you have time to do me a favor. My brother just called and told me my father's had another stroke and is in the hospital there in Sarnia. Could you drop in to see him? . . . That's great, Lambert! I really appreciate this. I have to leave on a trip and can't get over there . . . let me know how it comes out, will you?"

As I hung up, it struck me how God changes hearts and lives. During my teenage years I thought constantly of how I would kill my father someday for what he had done to me. Now I was asking a pastor friend to drop by to give him comfort and possibly talk to him about his soul. My brother Leroy, who had changed his name to Bill several years before, had called from Sarnia to tell me of Dad's latest stroke. This was the third one, all in the category doctors called "mild." But at age seventy-eight he was slowing down, and time was running out. This all happened before we made our move west to Vancouver.

With my Gideon friend's example in mind, I'd kept praying for my dad over the years, despite his lack of response to any mention of Christ or salvation. Dad wasn't hostile, just noncommittal. But he did seem to soften ever so slowly as we continued to try to keep in touch. I say "we" because Margie was probably more instrumental in bridging the gap between my father and me than I was. He liked Margie's friendly way and appreciated the cards she sent at Christmas and other occasions.

Betty had softened a little, too, but not as noticeably as my father. She was always ready to lash out if given reason, and when we goofed, we paid the price. In one instance, Margie and I were in the Sarnia area where I was doing some meetings for the Salvation Army. I remembered it was Betty's birthday and asked Margie to go with me to help buy her a present. We picked out a rather expensive broach costing over fifty dollars, got her a birthday card, and headed straight for the house with our gifts.

"I remembered it was your birthday," I said to Betty. "Hope you like it."

Betty looked slightly puzzled but went ahead and opened the gift, took out the broach and admired it, saying, "How lovely . . . how very nice."

Margie and I were silently congratulating ourselves on finally scoring points with Betty when she turned on me and practically snarled, "It's beautiful, you dumb cluck, but it's not my birthday. It's your *mother's* birthday! Don't you know the difference? Get out of my house . . . get out now!"

Mumbling apologies, Margie and I left as quickly as we could—without the broach. Angry as she was, Betty made it a point to keep it.

I couldn't believe I had made such a stupid error. Normally I have an excellent memory for dates, names, places, but somehow my wires had crossed. My goof gave my relationship to Betty and Dad a severe setback, and Betty never did let me forget my "stupid mistake."

After I called Lambert, I began wondering how he would do in contacting my dad because Betty could be such a handful. I wasn't surprised when Lambert called me back the next day saying he had gone to the hospital but hadn't been able to see my father because Betty had given him such a difficult time. He was going to try again in a day or two, hoping Betty might not be there when he dropped by.

I thanked Lambert for his concern and left to cover my weekend ministry assignment. I was busier than usual that summer of 1978, still managing the film rental department for E. P. Bookstore and doing ministry part-time. June came and went as I found myself constantly covering one crisis after the other. In July I attended the convention of Christian Booksellers Association in the U.S. and had just gotten back home, trying to catch up on my backlog of film rental work.

I had kept in touch with Bill and knew my father had gotten out of the hospital and was recovering. I wondered why Lambert Baptist had never called me back and made a mental note to give him a call soon to find out if he'd had any luck seeing my father and talking with him.

Early Friday morning, before seven o'clock, our household was just starting to function when the phone rang. It was my father, calling from the Toronto train station!

"Paul . . . I don't have much time. I'm headed for Sarnia and my train leaves by eight-thirty. Do you think you could come down and bring Margie and the girls?"

"I'll do my best, Dad, but it's twenty-five miles and traffic is heavy this time of morning. We'll leave in a few minutes."

Tina and Paula hadn't left yet for day camp, so I hustled them and Margie out to the van, and we plunged into rush hour traffic on the Don Valley Parkway. It was a typical Friday morning, and the parkway was more like a parking lot. When we finally pulled in at Union Station it was almost 8:30. We ran for the huge steel shuttered gates leading to the platforms from where all the trains leave, but when we got there it was closed. Off to the side was a smaller doorway, guarded by a man in uniform with a round cap. Trying to get my breath, I asked him, "Has the train left yet for Sarnia?"

"No, but it's leaving any minute. You can still get on, though, where are your tickets?"

"We don't have tickets, we're not going to Sarnia, but we've got to get on that train."

The uniformed man said, "Sorry, you can't get on without tickets."

I began arguing with him for what seemed like a long time when I happened to remember my ordination card in my wallet. "Look," I said as I showed him the card. "There's a man on that train who called me this morning. He has suffered a heart attack and has just been released from the hospital. I'm his son, and he wants to talk with me and my family."

The conductor looked at my card, which says I'm an ordained minister with the Open Door Evangelistic Association. It seemed forever before he said, "Well, I'll let you through, but your wife and children will have to stay here. If you get caught on the train when it pulls out, you'll have to pay for a ticket."

I squeezed past the conductor and called back to Margie, "If the train pulls out while I'm on it, I'll get off at Oakville and call you. But stay here until you're sure the train has left."

I ran down the platform between trains, still not sure which one was headed to Sarnia. I saw a conductor and shouted, "What train is going to Sarnia?"

"Next one down," he called. "You'd better hurry, it's pulling out."

I ran for the Sarnia train, jumped aboard, and a conductor immediately said, "Ticket, please."

"I don't have a ticket, I'm not taking this train, but I've got to talk to a man on board."

"This train's pulling out any second—"

"I know, but this man has had a heart attack. I'm a pastor, and I've got to talk to him!"

The conductor let me pass, and I walked hurriedly up the aisle of the car peering at the seats, trying to find my father. Then I saw Betty, who was seated facing me, and what looked like the back of my father's head as he sat facing her. Betty patted Dad on the knee, and he looked over his shoulder. When he saw me, he got up and started walking, almost running, up the aisle.

We met about halfway down and he said, "I'm glad to see you, Paul." That shocked me because he rarely called me Paul. But then the real shock came: my father hugged me! I could not remember any other time in my entire life when he had hugged me! For that matter, I couldn't remember another time when he had said, "I'm glad to see you."

Then we stood at arm's length for a few seconds and a million thoughts flashed through my mind. How old Dad was, and how small! I seemed to tower above him. On that terrible day when my mother died, he had looked like a giant as he beat and stomped on a little boy of seven. Now his wrinkled skin hung on his frame and his hair had thinned to almost nothing. He looked tired and I thought, *It must be the train ride.*

"Dad, are you all right?"

"Yeah, I'm fine, Paul, I'm fine. I just wanted to see you and Margie and the kids. Where are the kids?"

"The train's pulling out, and they wouldn't let all of us through. I was lucky to talk my way in here. I'm sorry."

"It's OK, it's OK . . . I'll see you all when you come to Sarnia."

"Yes, Dad, I'll be there in a couple of months, speaking at Temple Baptist."

"Yeah, I already know about that . . . I know all about it . . . I'll see you then." Then he looked into my face and said, "It's OK, Paul, it's OK. I love you, and I'll see you soon." Then he kissed me on the cheek! I could see the tears in his eyes, and I knew I had tears in mine. The flat grey stare was gone, and in its place his eyes glistened as if they had been washed clean from within.

"I love you too, Dad," I managed with my voice breaking. "You're sure everything's OK?"

"Yeah, things are going to be fine. . . ."

The train lurched, and he struggled to keep his balance. I knew I had to get off, so I hugged him again and gave his shoulder a final pat as I turned back down the aisle and he turned back toward his seat.

I waved to Betty, and she smiled slightly and waved back. Just before I left the car, I looked back one more time. My father had reached his seat, and he was looking back too. His eyes still glistened with tears—my father, who had always been too tough to cry and who had taught me to be the same that day so long ago when he screamed, "For cryin' out loud! Shut up, you stupid kid. Real men don't cry; babies cry!"

I really don't remember how I got off the train, back down the platform, and through the gate to where Margie and the girls were waiting. I kept saying, "My father hugged me, he kissed me, he said he loved me, and he had tears in his eyes!"

"Are you going to be all right?" Margie asked anxiously.

"Yes . . . I'm OK. . . . I'm OK. Why don't you just drop me off at work and go on home with the children?"

It was only a few blocks from Union Station to the E. P. Bookstore, and I went downstairs to my office where I found Jack Scruton who had been my friend at EP for years. Jack was the one who had covered for me on the Saturday when I went on my first date with Margie. I told him what happened, and I started to cry again. Jack went out and got me a cup of coffee and tried to help me get through the day. I never got much done, however, as my emotions and thoughts kept spinning crazily. That evening Margie and I talked about my father and what had happened.

"I know it's been a shock, Paul, but what wonderful news!" Margie observed as we got ready for bed. "Now maybe you can have a chance to talk to your dad about the Lord."

I went back to work on Saturday to try to make up for my "lost" day on Friday. On Sunday we went to church, and I mentioned my meeting with my father to our pastor, Gordon Heath. He prayed with me, thanking God for the breakthrough. Gordon was a Scotsman, too, from the Hebrides, and he knew how hard it was to reach a Scot. We prayed that my father would come to the service when I preached in Sarnia a few weeks hence, and that God would give me wisdom to point him toward Christ.

On Monday morning a bit after eight o'clock, as I was on my way out the door to go to work, Betty telephoned. She didn't try to prepare me for her news but just blurted out, "LaVern, you'd better come home! Your father just died in his sleep!"

I'm not sure what I did next. Margie says I screamed, and she came running down the stairs to find me beating on the kitchen table with the phone dangling from its hook on the wall. I was moaning, "He's dead. . . . He's dead."

Margie asked, "Who's dead?"

"My father's dead. I knew it . . . I knew it."

Margie tried to comfort me, and I heard her soothing voice, "Stop it. Stop it, now! Stop it."

Margie picked up the receiver and began talking to Betty. "Yes, we'll come. . . . We'll leave today." Then she turned to me and asked, "Will you do the church service?"

"No, I can't, but I'll get somebody to do it. I can't do it."

We got Tina and Paula dressed and were on the road in less than an hour. Luckily, one of the young girls in our neighborhood who frequently baby-sat for us was able to go along. She would stay with the girls at the motel while we attended the funeral. Margie and I had agreed that we didn't want the girls at the service.

We got into Sarnia late that afternoon, left the girls with the sitter at the motel, and went on over to the house. Bill and Tommy were there. Tommy had been suffering with a disease of the eyes for years and was practically blind. Kathleen, Jimmy, and Bobby weren't around. They all lived in western provinces, and I thought they might be arriving later.

I spent Tuesday trying to find a minister to conduct Dad's service. First I called Lambert Baptist at the church but was told he would be on vacation for at least another week. The church secretary suggested that I try calling Delos Scott, an evangelist who was filling in for Lambert while he was gone. Margie and I got together with Pastor Scott, and he wanted to know a few things about my father. He asked Margie to tell him some good things, and she replied, "I don't know—you'd better ask Paul. I never heard anything good . . . isn't that awful?"

"Well," said Delos, "we've got to say *something* good about him."

I shared what had happened the previous Friday—how I managed to see my father on the train, how he hugged me and kissed me and said, "Paul, it's OK, I love you." That seemed to satisfy Delos, and he said he'd see us at the service to be held the next day at a funeral home in Sarnia.

The next day at the funeral, relatives from both sides of the family were there. They congregated in separate areas, most of them talking in hushed tones, but one bitter voice could be heard above everyone's. Betty was turning the air blue because Kathleen, Jimmy, and Bobby had all refused to come. Donna, who had moved from Toronto to Sarnia, also refused, even though she lived only a few blocks from the funeral parlor.

"No-good kids," snapped Betty. "You'd think they'd at least show up for their own father's funeral."

The service was brief, and I really don't remember much of what Delos Scott said. Margie told me later that it was a good message, challenging those present about where they would spend eternity.

Lost in my thoughts, I sat through the service, asking, *Why, Dad, why? Why did you die now, when we were so close to finally getting to know one another? I was coming in just a few more weeks, and we could have talked and shared, and I could have introduced you to my Savior.*

It was a hot July afternoon, and at the graveside the sun beat down on us. Betty continued to complain bitterly because my father was buried next to my mother and there would be no room left in the family plot for her when she died. I just walked away. It really didn't make any difference to me where Dad was buried.

Afterward we all went over to my stepbrother David's house, and he and his wife, Dawn, hosted a time of refreshments and talking. It was then that I learned from Bill that my father had made an extensive trip west just before he had returned home, managing to get in touch with Kathleen but failing to find Jimmy and Bobby. He had come through Toronto on his way back to Sarnia because those were the only train connections he could get. That's why he had called and gotten me down to the train station that morning.

I would always be grateful for what had happened. At least I had the memory of hearing my father say he loved me. And I would always feel his kiss on my cheek, his arms around me, and see the tears in his eyes.

A little over two months later, early in October, I was back in Sarnia to preach at the Temple Baptist Church. I had arranged to handle this weekend of meetings alone, so I dropped Margie off at the farm in Tillsonburg on the way to Sarnia. Andy and I were in rare form on Friday night as we did a program for teenagers. We also came back to do a Saturday afternoon program for children and another program for youth on Saturday night.

The hotel where I stayed turned out to have a very familiar view. As I looked out my window, I could see the Catholic church and school right across the street. It was then I realized that my hotel was standing on the site of the old Sarnia City Jail! And my room was in approximately the same spot my cell had been over thirty years before, when I had been arrested for robbery and murder!

On Sunday morning I presented "Gospel Magic with a Message" for the entire Sunday school and came back the second hour to do it for the junior church. I was also scheduled to speak that night at the church in a program that would be broadcast locally on the radio. Following the morning services, Lambert Baptist invited me over to the house for dinner, and we got caught up on things. He told me he was enjoying his new ministry after leaving the church at Tillsonburg and taking the Temple Baptist pastorate. Then I shared about my father's quick visit to Sarnia and our meeting on the train. I mentioned how much it meant to me to have Dad say he loved me and give me a hug and a kiss with tears in his eyes, and how he had been looking forward to coming to tonight's service to hear me preach.

"Who knows?" I speculated. "Dad might have come to the Savior tonight had he lived to be here."

Lambert sat straight up, as if he had been jabbed by a big pin, and said, "Didn't you know?"

"Didn't I know what?"

"When you called me last May and asked me to visit your father in the hospital, we finally did get in to see him. Your cousin Wes was with me, and we talked with your father for quite awhile. Before we left, your father became a Christian. I thought Delos Scott knew all this, and I was sure he would—"

Stunned, I interrupted Lambert, "Wait a minute, wait a minute. You mean he actually made a decision to receive Christ as his Savior?"

"Oh, absolutely. I led him through the plan of salvation myself, and after he got out of the hospital, he would stop by often to talk with me, pray, and get some spiritual guidance. That's when he decided to make that trip out west, trying to contact some of your brothers and sisters. He wanted to heal old wounds, if he could. And when he got back, he planned to be baptized during tonight's services before you spoke. You say he never mentioned this when he met you on the train that day?"

"He was planning to be baptized?" I couldn't believe it! It was all too much! My father had been a Christian that day we met on the train . . . of course! What else could have changed him? Who else could have brought tears to his eyes and love to his voice and touch other than Jesus Christ himself?

"Yes—I'm sure I have that correct. I was going to call you and ask you to help with your father's baptism. Just a minute, I've got some material . . ."

He left the room and came back and showed me some papers that plainly said Albert Powers had been scheduled for baptismal classes at Temple Baptist Church during the month of September and that he planned to join the church after being baptized.

I hurried back to my hotel and phoned Margie at the farm to tell her what Lambert had said.

"Paul, that's wonderful!" she said excitedly. "No wonder he came to Toronto and wanted to see you. It was because of what had happened. Now it all makes sense."

"Yes, it does make sense. Finally, it's all making sense . . . I'll see you tonight, Sweetheart. I'll drive over to the farm after the service."

That evening I sat there watching the baptismal service that was held before I was to preach. I tried to imagine how it would have been to have my father there and how wonderful it would have been to baptize him myself. I felt pangs of regret because now that would never be, but at the same time I was comforted by realizing that baptism would not have saved Dad. The decision he had made in his hospital bed had brought him to salvation, and the change in his attitude and actions had proved that his profession of faith was genuine.

Then it was time for me to preach. I stood up at the pulpit before an audience that included some of my aunts and uncles and one of the kids who had gone to school with me at Hannah Memorial. There was also a family that used to live in our neighborhood. They had heard I was coming, and they had made a special effort to come hear me that evening.

But my stepmother was not there. Despite my father's decision, Betty never changed. She was still rejecting the Savior that she had turned away from in her youth.

"Good evening," I said. "I've never preached here before, but I have been in your church." I could see puzzled looks on the faces of some of the longtime members of Temple Baptist, and then I continued, "As a boy, I was in a gang that used to rob your church from time to time. We would come when no one was around, break into the office, and 'take up an offering.' As I recall, you were quite generous."

When the laughter died away, I spoke for almost an hour about growing up in Sarnia, becoming part of a gang, serving time in prison, and how I was saved. Then I told them a bit about the wonderful family and ministry God had given me. I closed by sharing about hearing Dad say "I love you" on a Friday, then learning of his death the next Monday. But while my father was dead, yet did he live because he had come to Christ through the ministry of their pastor.

I didn't stick around long after the service. I jumped into my car and headed for Tillsonburg to be with Margie and the girls. The night was frosty—the first snowfall would be coming soon—but I drove with the windows down. The biting air smelled and tasted good.

As the miles rolled by, I thought of all the fathers I had had. There had been Dad Adams back in Frankford, when I was a hate-filled teenager. He and Mom Adams had adopted me—not officially, but in a much more vital way—into their hearts, and they had played a key role in my life. Both of them were gone now—Dad had died in 1966 and Mom had lived on for another five years. I thanked God that both of them had been able to come to our wedding, and I smiled as I thought of that first day we had met: they hadn't cared about my past—only what God would do with my future!

Then I thought of Dad Fishback—Margie's father—who had died suddenly just eight months before. He went the way he would have preferred to go, hard at work one morning at his farm. According to old-time residents of Tillsonburg, his funeral was the largest they had ever seen. Hundreds of people turned out to pay respects to a man who was known and respected throughout western Ontario, not only for his dairy cattle but for his integrity.

Margie was devastated by her father's death. She felt particularly bad about not having seen him all summer because we were so busy with ministry. The heart attack had been sudden and totally unexpected, and he was gone before an ambulance could even be summoned.

Dad Fishback's death shook me, too, and I realized I missed him even more than I missed Dad Adams. We had grown very close since I had married Margie some eleven years before. We often took walks together across his farm, and we would talk—about life, about struggles, about the farm, the cattle, his daughter, his hopes for his family, or some point a Christian broadcaster had made in his sermon on the radio.

Dad Fishback had never been much for church. Something had happened long before that had turned him off and he never attended, but he always encouraged his wife and children to go. They had always tithed, whatever their income was, and I remember once he told me that a lot of pastors reminded him of a woman with a huge pile of laundry, studying her washing machine to figure out how it worked. He said, "If pastors spent less time studying what's wrong with the other denominations and just spent more time using the Bible's message, they'd be more effective."

Margie was always bothered by the fact that her father had never joined the church and made an "official profession of faith." But there is no question in my mind that Dad Fishback is in the Kingdom.

He was a quiet, stern man but a true and honest friend—and a loving father. He loved his children deeply, and he loved me as if I were one of them. He had his faults, but he is still my model of what a successful father should be.

As I turned off the main highway and headed down the country road to the Fishback farm, my thoughts came back to my own father. I had never really known him, and now it seemed as if I had been cheated out of the chance. But then I thanked God that he had given me that single precious experience of feeling Dad's touch of love and hearing him say, "It's OK, it's OK. . . ."

And it *was* OK—despite the beatings, the curses, the liquor, the cold indifference, even the hatred. That was all part of a past that had been canceled out by something far more power-ful. God's love had broken down the unscalable wall between my father and me. I had spent only a few moments with my father on that train, but we would have all eternity to talk together and make up for the lost years he had created.

On earth we must live with what human beings create, and it is often difficult and painful. But in heaven we will live with what God has created. We will cast our crowns—and our trials—at Jesus' feet and honor and glorify him. I knew God would allow me some privileged and special moments with my father.

Meanwhile, there were more children to reach . . . more LaVerns, Tommys, Donnas, and Davids who needed a loving touch and a kindly word. Some of them were crying aloud, others were weeping silently within, but they all needed the same thing—the love of Jesus.

As I turned up the Fishback driveway, I could imagine my father sitting around the Throne, looking down and saying, "For cryin' out loud! . . . It's OK, Paul . . . I love you . . . I'll see you soon!"

A SPECIAL WORD ABOUT CHILDREN

Unless we reach their hearts today,
They will break our hearts tomorrow!

These words have been our slogan for almost twenty-five years. During that time a generation of children has grown up, and we have seen personally the tremendous difference between children who are reached for Christ and those who are not. If reading this book has prompted you to ask, "What can I do to help reach the hearts of children today?" we offer these suggestions:

Children need someone who will listen. *Don't be too busy to pay attention to their questions, hopes, fears, and accomplishments. While writing this book I spoke to a group of children in a Sunday school program and taught them a trick involving two small loops. I also taught them how to use the trick as an object lesson while sharing the gospel in a brief and simple way. Two sisters, ages nine and seven, were especially interested in learning the trick and the correct way to explain the object lesson. They came up after the program and asked for more help.*

While I was working with the two little girls, a short, balding man came striding over and began talking to one of the women in charge of the Sunday school. The older sister saw the man and ran over to him, tugging at his sleeve excitedly. "Excuse me, Daddy! Can I show you my new trick?"

"Yes, yes, in a minute," he replied, barely looking at her. The girl waited patiently for a few minutes, then tugged at her father's sleeve again. "Excuse me, Daddy, but can I show you this?"

"I don't have time now," he said irritably.

"You say that all the time!" the little girl protested.

"Not here!" said her father sternly.

"Daddy, it just takes thirty seconds!"

By now the father saw us watching, sighed, and said, "OK— let's see it."

The little girl did her trick beautifully, manipulating the two small loops while she shared the lines of gospel witness I had taught her. But she seemed to be going too slowly for her father, who said, "Get to the point!" She finished the trick as quickly as she could and waited for his response.

"Neat!" was all Dad said—and he turned quickly away to talk to somebody else. This man is in full-time Christian ministry, and as he hurried off, his young daughters looked at each other with expressions of frustration and disappointment. Then they walked slowly away.

I've seen those same looks on the faces of literally thousands of children over the years. They are looks that say, "Dad (or Mom) isn't interested. He goes through the motions, but he doesn't really have time to pay attention to us."

As I shared in chapter 17, we had to learn this lesson ourselves when our own daughter Paula, who was only five at the time, let us know that we were always too busy—off on crusades or other teaching ministries. What little Paula said changed our lives, and we have taken special concentrated, planned-for time with her and Tina ever since. If Christian parents would take time to be aware of and really listen to their children, the impact would be inestimable!

Children need to be taken more seriously. *If you work in Sunday school, AWANA, or any other children's ministry, teach children, yes, but also give them opportunities to use what they learn. Try to find ways they can serve and use their own spiritual gifts. The Bible says nothing about spiritual gifts being limited to adults. Children have them, too, so why do we seem to make them sit until they're teenagers or even young adults before we* *finally believe they have something to say or contribute?*

I know children can serve in the church and in its various programs, not just sit in classes. They have gifts and talents that should be developed now. That's why we emphasize a program called H.I.T.—Helpers in Training. We want to encourage children to do more than come to church to be taught and entertained. They can be involved in ministry and outreach.

I believe that children in the church have been overtaught and underused. We see it all the time during crusades in churches and at camps. People will tell us, "I didn't realize children could memorize so much in such a short time," or, "I really didn't think that kids that young could do anything practical or useful."

We see ourselves as having the gift of helping children find their places in the body as they develop their own gifts. After twenty-five years of children's ministry, we still don't believe we have all the answers—who does? Because the worldly system changes its point of attack from year to year, we are constantly on the alert, working one on one with children whenever possible. First we tell them the old, old story and lead them to Christ; then we encourage those who are born again to be equipped to minister to other children—or even their parents.

Children have potential that must be recognized. *Ask the Holy Spirit to help you see the potential in each precious child who may come within your scope of influence. In our human wisdom we often say, "That little girl is too young for that," or, "That little boy couldn't possibly understand this." As I shared in this book, children can understand a great deal more than we give them credit for.*

Children also have individual hurts that can be dealt with now. There is no need to wait until they become adults to help heal things that happened to them when they were very young. If someone could have talked to me the way I am able to talk to children today, perhaps I could have gotten rid of some of my hurt much sooner. Because I had to wait until I was twenty to find Christ, I'm still dealing with the things that happened to me when I was very small.

I know adults can learn from children. I often close my eyes and think of the thousands of kids over the years who have helped me personally with their questioning, their searching, and their longings. And I often think about how I almost missed all those blessings.

Right after Margie and I were married, people from our church approached me about teaching a Sunday school class of younger children. I refused. I had the knowledge, and I had quite a bit of experience in speaking to teenagers, but little kids just plain bugged me. I thought they were too young to under- stand anything and that dealing with them was more or less a glorified baby-sitting process—a waste of time.

But God had other plans. He kept bringing small children across my path in one way or another. I learned that, as the apostle Paul says, "the body is not one member, but many." Could Paul have been thinking about children when he talked about the weaker members of the body? Perhaps. At the same time, I've seen children who have studied the Word of God who were far stronger spiritually than some adults who have been in the church for years.

I recall being at a fireside service at a summer camp, and a little boy got up and said, "I got saved Thursday! Jesus has changed me for life!" That's what it's all about—to have Jesus change us for life.

Our prayer as the Powers family is, "Break us, Lord; break us and lead us to the little children—these little people. Take everything out of us that would prevent the children from seeing Jesus first. May Jesus be in our actions, our words, and our touch as we reach, train, encourage, and love these little people."

My wife, Margie, has written many beautiful poems, but none catches the spirit of how we see children better than "The Soul of a Child":

> *The soul of a child is the loveliest flower*
> *That grows in the Garden of God.*
> *Its climb is from weakness to knowledge and power,*
> *To the sky from the clay to the clod.*
> *To beauty and sweetness it grows under care,*
> *Neglected, 'tis ragged and wild.*
> *'Tis a plant that is tender, but wondrously rare,*
> *The sweet wistful soul of a child.*

May the "flowers" in your particular garden receive the best kind of care. Don't neglect a single one. Remember: "Unless we reach their hearts today, they will break our hearts tomorrow!"

In God's love for children,
Paul and Margie Powers